PREVENTION OF MONEY LAUNDERING ACT 2002- SUPREME COURT'S LATEST CASE LAWS

CASE NOTES- FACTS- FINDINGS OF APEX COURT JUDGES & CITATIONS

JAYPRAKASH BANSILAL SOMANI

Dedicated

To

All the Past & Present Judges of the Supreme Court of India.

Salute to their wisdom.

Salute to their interpretation of Law.

Salute to their elaborative judgement writing.

SUPREME COURT OF INDIA

॰ৎ৩॰

Contents

Preface — *vii*

Acknowledgements — *ix*

1. V. Senthil Balaji Vs. The State Represented By Deputy Director And Ors. (07.08.2023 - SC) : MANU/SC/0839/2023 — 1

2. Anoop Bartaria And Ors. Vs. Dy. Director Enforcement Directorate And Ors. (21.04.2023 - SC) : MANU/SC/0438/2023 — 7

3. Enforcement Directorate, Government Of India Vs. Kapil Wadhawan And Ors. (27.03.2023 - SC) : MANU/SC/0329/2023 — 10

4. The Directorate Of Enforcement Vs. M. Gopal Reddy And Ors. (24.02.2023 - SC) : MANU/SC/0166/2023 — 15

5. Rana Ayyub Vs. Directorate Of Enforcement Through Its Assistant Director (07.02.2023 - SC) : MANU/SC/0096/2023 — 18

6. Bikram Chatterji And Ors. Vs. Union Of India (UOI) And Ors. (07.11.2022 - SC) : MANU/SC/1484/2022 — 22

7. J. Sekar Vs. Directorate Of Enforcement (05.05.2022 - SC) : MANU/SC/0596/2022 — 28

8. Opto Circuit India Ltd. Vs. Axis Bank And Ors. (03.02.2021 - SC) : MANU/SC/0049/2021 — 31

9. P. Chidambaram Vs. Directorate Of Enforcement (04.12.2019 - SC) : MANU/SC/1670/2019 — 35

10. P. Chidambaram Vs. Directorate Of Enforcement (05.09.2019 - SC) : MANU/SC/1209/2019 — 39

11. Nikesh Tarachand Shah Vs. Union Of India (UOI) And Ors. (23.11.2017 - SC) : MANU/SC/1480/2017 — 45

12. Rohit Tandon Vs. The Enforcement Directorate (10.11.2017 - SC) : MANU/SC/1403/2017 — 50

13. Gautam Kundu Vs. Manoj Kumar, Govt. Of India (16.12.2015 - SC) : MANU/SC/1453/2015 — 54

Contents

14. P. Mohanraj And Ors. Vs. Shah Brothers Ispat Pvt. Ltd. (01.03.2021 - SC) : MANU/SC/0132/2021 — 62

15. Union Of India (UOI) Vs. Hassan Ali Khan And Ors. (30.09.2011 - SC) : MANU/SC/1144/2011 — 70

16. Suborno Bose Vs. Enforcement Directorate And Ors. (05.03.2020 - SC) : MANU/SC/0285/2020 — 73

17. Union Of India (UOI) And Ors. Vs. Premier Limited And Ors. (29.01.2019 - SC) : MANU/SC/0094/2019 — 77

18. Union Of India (UOI) And Ors. Vs. S. Srinivasan (21.05.2012 - SC) : MANU/SC/0496/2012 — 82

19. Thirumalai Chemicals Limited Vs. Union Of India (UOI) And Ors. (11.04.2011 - SC) : MANU/SC/0427/2011 — 88

20. Union Of India (UOI) Vs. Ashok Kumar Sharma And Ors. (28.08.2020 - SC) : MANU/SC/0648/2020 — 92

21. Maars Software International Ltd. And Ors. Vs. Union Of India (UOI) And Ors. (22.04.2019 - SC) : MANU/SC/0579/2019 — 96

Adv. Jayprakash Somani's Videos on Law — 99

List of Adv. Jayprakash Somani's Published Books — 105

Adv Jayprakash Somani's Online Legal & Import Export Courses — 109

Preface

Dear Learned Advocates of Trial Court, High court and Supreme Court, Corporate and Individuals.

I am very delighted to provide you a book on **PREVENTION OF MONEY LAUNDERING ACT 2002- SUPREME COURT'S LATEST CASE LAWS**

In this book you will get...

1. Name of the Case i. e. Cause title

2. Relevant Sections discussed in the case

3. Hon'ble Judges/Coram of the case

4.Number of PDF Pages in Original Judgement of the case

5. All available Citations of the case

6. Case Note with appeal allowed/ dismissed or disposed off

7. Facts of the case

8. Hon'ble Apex Court's findings, while dismissing/allowing or disposing the appeal

9. Ratio Decidendi if any.

My special thanks to Manupatra, because of their web portal I can compile this book in well manner. I am also thankful to Notion Press to support me to publish & market this book throughout the Country. Thanks to my Juniors, Advocate Colleagues & Insolvency Professional Colleagues to support me in this venture.

Adv. Manoj Kumar Chowdhary & Adv. Shruti Kriti has helped me a lot to compile this book. I hope this book will add some value addition in the wealth of your legal knowledge. Your positive feedbacks will boost me to compile/ write further books & negative feedbacks will improve my skills. Kindly send your valuable feedbacks by email.

Thanks with Regards,

Jayprakash B. Somani

Advocate, Supreme Court of India

Email: jaysomani64@gmail.com

Web Site:www.jayprakashsomani.com

Call: 9322188701, 8459194576

Acknowledgements

Printed & Published by
Notion Press
No. 8, 3rd Cross Street,
CIT Colony, Mylapore,
Chennai, Tamil Nadu- 600004

જી

Managed by
Jayprakash Somani Advocates & Solicitors
Law Firm for Supreme Court of India
Delhi Office
B- 851, 1st Floor, Shivaji Marg, New Ashok Nagar, Delhi 110096.
Call: 9322188701, 8459194576
Supreme Court Chamber
312, 3rd Floor, M. C. Setalvad Block, In front of 'D' Gate, Bhagwan Das
Road, Supreme Court of India, New Delhi 110001
Contact: 8459194576, 9811011747
www.jayprakashsomani.com

જી

Download our app to get access to our Free Videos, Free Bare Acts, Free
Study Material in Legal as well as International Business Regime.
Android App Link ;-https://clpandrea.page.link/cmSm
Ios APp Link :-https://apps.apple.com/us/app/classplus/id1324522260
Login with org code ;- (qywzji)
Web Link ;-https://qywzji.courses.store/
Opportunity for Lawyers/ Social Workers to get Supreme Court Law
Firm JSAS's authorised centre at District Level.
Kindly Message or Call to: 9322188701

જી

Books are available online in India
1. **Notion Press:**https://notionpress.com/author/jayprakash_somani
2. **Amazon:**https://www.amazon.in/s?k=jayprakash+somani
3. **Flipkart:**https://www.flipkart.com/search?q=Jayprakash%20Somani

ACKNOWLEDGEMENTS

Books are available online at International Market
4. Amazon International: https://www.amazon.com/s?k=jayprakash+somani
5. Amazon United Kingdom: https://www.amazon.co.uk/s?k=jayprakash+somani
6. E-Books/Kindle edition at National & International Level: https://www.amazon.in/s?k=jaypraksh+somani

೮೨

I

V. Senthil Balaji vs. The State represented by Deputy Director and Ors. (07.08.2023 - SC) : MANU/SC/0839/2023

Relative Section:

Code of Civil Procedure, 1908 (CPC) - Section 144;

Code of Criminal Procedure, 1898 (CrPC) - Section 4(1), Section 61, Section 167(1), Section 167(2), Section 344; Code of Criminal Procedure, 1973 (CrPC) - Section 2(h),Section 3,Section 4,Section 4(2), Section 5,Section 21,Section 41,Section 41A,Section 50,Section 57, Section 61,Section 167,Section 167(1),Section 167(2),Section 173,Section 190(1),Section 309,Section 469, Section 470;

Constitution of India - Article 21, Article 22, Article 22(1), Article 22(2), Article 226;

Customs Act, 1962 - Section 102, Section 104, Section 104(2), Section 132, Section 133, Section 135,Section 135A, Section 136, Section 137;

Foreign Exchange Regulation Act, 1973 - Section 35, Section 35(2),Section 61(ii); Indian Evidence Act, 1872 - Section 25; Narcotic Drugs And Psychotropic Substances Act, 1985 - Section 53A, Section 67;

Prevention Of Money-laundering Act, 2002 - Section 3, Section 4, Section 9, Section 17,Section 19,Section 19(1), Section 19(3), Section 44, Section 44(1), Section 45, Section 46, Section 62, Section 65

Hon'ble Judges/Coram: A.S. Bopanna and M.M. Sundresh, JJ

Equivalent Citation: 2023(4)CTC758, 2023/INSC/677, 2023(4)KLT814, 2023 (2) MWN (CR.) 633

Number of Pages in the Original Judgment: 53

Case Reference:

Central Bureau of Investigation, Special Investigation Cell-I, New Delhi v. Anupam J. Kulkarni MANU/SC/0335/1992; Directorate of Enforcement v. Deepak Mahajan and Ors. MANU/SC/0422/1994; Ashok Munilal Jain and Ors. v. Assistant Director, Directorate of Enforcement MANU/SC/1846/2017; The State of Maharashtra and Ors. v. Tasneem Rizwan Siddiquee MANU/SC/0940/2018; Saurabh Kumar v. Jailor, Koneila Jail MANU/SC/0626/2014; Manubhai Ratilal Patel Tr. Ushaben v. State of Gujarat and Ors. MANU/SC/0800/2012; Tasneem Rizwan Siddiquee v. The State of Maharashtra and Ors. MANU/MH/0584/2018; Arnesh Kumar v. State of Bihar MANU/SC/0559/2014; Premium Granites and Ors. v. State of Tamil Nadu and Ors. MANU/SC/0466/1994; Sukhwinder Pal Bipan Kumar and Ors. v. State of Punjab and Ors. MANU/SC/0071/1981; CBI v. Vikas Mishra MANU/SC/0342/2023; Ahmed Noormohmed Bhatti v. State of Gujarat and Ors. MANU/SC/0207/2005; Satender Kumar Antil v. CBI MANU/SC/0851/2022; Manzoor Ali Khan v. Union of India (UOI) MANU/SC/0668/2014; Romesh Chandra Mehta v. State of West Bengal MANU/SC/0282/1968; Union of India (UOI) v. Padam Narain Aggarwal and Ors. MANU/SC/4230/2008; Tofan Singh v. State of Tamil Nadu MANU/SC/0797/2020; State of Rajasthan and Ors. v. Basant Agrotech (India) Ltd. MANU/SC/1261/2013; Sundeep Kumar Bafna v. State of Maharashtra and Ors. MANU/SC/0239/2014; Bharat Damodar Kale and Ors. v. State of A.P. MANU/SC/0794/2003; Rashmi Kumar v. Mahesh Kumar Bhada MANU/SC/1052/1997; Indore Development Authority v. Manoharlal and Ors. MANU/SC/0300/2020; Mritunjoy Pani and Ors. v. Narmanda Bala Sasmal and Ors. MANU/SC/0357/1961; Mahadeo Savlaram Shelke and Ors. v. Puna Municipal Corporation and Ors. MANU/SC/0673/1995; Amarjeet Singh and Ors. v. Devi Ratan and Ors. MANU/SC/1843/2009; Ram Krishna Verma and Ors. v. State of U.P. and Ors. MANU/SC/0496/1992; Shiv Shankar and Ors. v. Board of Directors, U.P.S.R.T.C. and Ors. MANU/SC/1088/1995; GTC Industries Limited v. Union of India (UOI) and Ors. MANU/SC/0189/1998; Jaipur Municipal Corporation v. C.L. Mishra MANU/SC/2511/2005; Grindlays

Bank Limited v. Income Tax Officer, Calcutta and Ors. MANU/SC/0276/1980; Karnataka Rare Earth and Ors. v. The Senior Geologist, Department of Mines and Geology and Ors. MANU/SC/0057/2004; A.R. Antulay v. R.S. Nayak and Ors. MANU/SC/0002/1988; State of Gujarat v. Ramprakash P. Puri and Ors. MANU/SC/0157/1969; Keshardeo Chamria v. Radha Kissen Chamria and Ors. MANU/SC/0006/1952; South Eastern Coalfields Ltd. v. State of M.P. and Ors. MANU/SC/0807/2003; Zafar Khan and Ors. v. Board of Revenue, U.P. and Ors. MANU/SC/0251/1984; A. Arunagiri v. S.P. Rathinasami MANU/TN/0311/1970; M. Ravindran v. The Intelligence Officer, Directorate of Revenue Intelligence MANU/SC/0788/2020; Uday Mohanlal Acharya v. State of Maharashtra MANU/SC/0222/2001; Maneka Gandhi v. Union of India (UOI) and Ors. MANU/SC/0133/1978; Rakesh Kumar Paul v. State of Assam MANU/SC/0993/2017; S. Kasi v. State MANU/SC/0491/2020; Satyajit Ballulbhai Desai and Ors. v. State of Gujarat MANU/SC/1282/2012; Aswini Kumar Ghosh and Ors. v. Arabinda Bose and Ors. MANU/SC/0022/1952; Jugalkishore Saraf v. Raw Cotton Co. Ltd. MANU/SC/0005/1955; Kanai Lal Sur v. Paramnidhi Sadhukhan MANU/SC/0097/1957; K.T.M.T.M. Abdul Kayoom and Ors. v. Commissioner of Income Tax MANU/SC/0207/1961; Union of India (UOI) v. Amrit Lal Manchanda and Ors. MANU/SC/0133/2004; Satya Pal Singh v. State of M.P. and Ors. MANU/SC/1119/2015; Dwarka Prasad v. Dwarka Das Saraf MANU/SC/0505/1975; S. Sundaram Pillai and Ors. v. `R. Pattabiraman and Ors. MANU/SC/0387/1985; Chaganti Satyanarayana and Ors. v. State of Andhra Pradesh MANU/SC/0165/1986

Case Note:

Criminal - Investigation - Police custody - Section 19 of Prevention of Money Laundering Act, 2002 (PMLA)- The principal issue in present case is only on the remand in favour of the investigating agency - Whether Appellant was duly produced before the learned Principal Sessions Judge in compliance with Section 19 of the PMLA, 2002

Facts:

The Appellant is a Cabinet Minister of the State of Tamil Nadu. A case was registered in Enforcement Case Information Report by the Respondent No. 1 against the Appellant and others. It was followed by summons requiring the attendance of the Appellant. Further summons were issued. A search was conducted by the Authorised Officer invoking Section 17 of the PMLA, 2002 at his premises. Finding that the Appellant was not extending adequate cooperation, the Authority had invoked Section 19 of the PMLA, 2002 by way of an arrest on 14.06.2023. After the Scheduled Offence went through an elongated judicial journey, it is the turn of the Enforcement Case Information Report under the Prevention of Money Laundering Act, 2002 ("the PMLA, 2002"). What is under challenge are the orders passed by the majority of the Judges, when a reference was made on a difference of opinion by the Division Bench of the Madras High Court, while dealing with a Writ Petition filed seeking a writ of Habeas Corpus in pursuance of an arrest made, followed by a remand to the judicial custody, and then to the authority concerned. The principal issue is only on the remand in favour of the investigating agency, without seeking any specific prayer challenging the remand orders, though additional grounds were raised. It is submitted that, there is no power vested under the PMLA, 2002 to seek custody in favour of an authorized officer. Such an authorized officer is not a police officer and therefore, Section 167(2) of the Code of Criminal Procedure, 1973 ("the CrPC, 1973"), with particular reference to a remand in his favour, is not available. Custody Under Section 167(2) of the CrPC can only be in favour of a police officer and not any other agency. There is no investigation under the PMLA, 2002 since it is to be taken as synonymous with inquiry. After the completion of 24 hours from the arrest, there cannot be further custody in favour of an officer. Being a beneficial legislation, non-compliance of Section 41A of the CrPC would vitiate the orders of remand. The learned Principal Sessions Judge passed a cryptic order ignoring the clear non-compliance of Section 19 of the PMLA, 2002.

Held, while dismissing the appeal

1. This case has got a chequered history with the pendulum swinging in favour of one side to another. The order rejecting the bail has attained finality. [80]

2. A writ of Habeas Corpus was moved questioning the arrest made. When it was taken up for hearing on a mentioning, the next day by the Court, the Appellant was duly produced before the learned Principal Sessions Judge in compliance with Section 19 of the PMLA, 2002. The custody thus becomes judicial as he was duly forwarded by the Respondents. Therefore, even on the date of hearing before the High Court there was no cause for filing the Writ Petition being HCP No. 1021 of 2023. Added to that, an order of remand was passed on 14.06.2023 itself. The two remand orders passed by the Court, as recorded in the preceding paragraphs, depict a clear application of mind. Despite additional grounds having been raised, they being an afterthought, we have no hesitation in holding that the only remedy open to the Appellant is to approach the

appropriate Court under the Statute. This was obviously not done. Appellant was very conscious about his rights and that is the reason why, by way of an application he even opposed the remand. [81]

3. As rightly contended by the learned Solicitor General the scheme and object of the PMLA, 2002 being a sui generis legislation is distinct. Present Court find adequate compliance of Section 19 of the PMLA, 2002 which contemplates a rigorous procedure before making an arrest. The learned Principal Sessions Judge did take note of the said fact by passing a reasoned order. The Appellant was accordingly produced before the Court and while he was in its custody, a judicial remand was made. As it is a reasoned and speaking order, the Appellant ought to have questioned it before the appropriate forum. Present Court is only concerned with the remand in favour of the Respondents. Therefore, even on that ground, a writ of Habeas Corpus is not maintainable as the arrest and custody have already been upheld by way of rejection of the bail application. [82]

4. The Appellant continues to be in judicial custody. Admittedly, physical custody has not been given to the Respondents. Admission of the Appellant to the hospital of his choice cannot be termed as a physical custody in favour of the Respondents. Custody could not be taken on the basis of the interim order passed by the High Court which certainly shall not come in the way of calculating the period of 15 days. An investigating agency is expected to be given a reasonable freedom to do it's part. To say that the Respondents ought to have examined the Appellant in the hospital, and that too with the permission of the doctors, can never be termed as an adequate compliance. [86]

5. Any order of the Court is not meant to affect a person adversely despite its ultimate conclusion in his favour. The doctrine actus curiae neminem gravabit would certainly apply in calculating the period of 15 days. [87]

6. When an arrestee is forwarded to the jurisdictional Magistrate Under Section 19(3) of the PMLA, 2002, no writ of Habeas Corpus would lie. Any plea of illegal arrest is to be made before such Magistrate since custody becomes judicial. Any non-compliance of the mandate of Section 19 of the PMLA, 2002 would ensure to the benefit of the person arrested. For such non- compliance, the Competent Court shall have the power to initiate action Under Section 62 of the PMLA, 2002. An order of remand has to be challenged only before a higher forum as provided under the Code of Criminal Procedure, 1973 when it depicts a due application of mind both on merit and compliance of Section 167(2) of the Code of Criminal Procedure,

1973 (CrPC) read with Section 19 of the PMLA 2002. Section 41A of the CrPC has got no application to an arrest made under the PMLA 2002. The maximum period of 15 days of police custody is meant to be applied to the entire period of investigation - 60 or 90 days, as a whole. The words "such custody" occurring in Section 167(2) of the CrPC would include not only a police custody but also that of other investigating agencies. The word "custody" Under Section 167(2) of the CrPC shall mean actual custody. Curtailment of 15 days of police custody by any extraneous circumstances, act of God, an order of Court not being the handy work of investigating agency would not act as a restriction. Section 167 of the CrPC is a bridge between liberty and investigation performing a fine balancing act. [88]

7. Appeals dismissed. [89]

8. The Registry is directed to place the matter before Hon'ble the Chief Justice of India for appropriate orders to decide the larger issue of the actual import of Section 167(2) of the Code of Criminal Procedure, 1973 as to whether the 15 days period of custody in favour of the police should be only within the first 15 days of remand or spanning over the entire period of investigation - 60 or 90 days, as the case may be, as a whole. [91]

Ratio Decidendi: When an arrestee is forwarded to the jurisdictional Magistrate under Section 19(3) of the PMLA, 2002, no writ of Habeas Corpus would lie.

II

Anoop Bartaria and Ors. vs. Dy. Director Enforcement Directorate and Ors. (21.04.2023 - SC) : MANU/SC/0438/2023

Relative Section:

Code of Criminal Procedure, 1973 (CrPC) - Section 155(2), Section 156(1), Section 482;

Companies Act, 1956;Constitution of India - Article 226; Finance (No. 2) Act, 2019;

Indian Penal Code, 1860 (IPC) - Section 120B,Section 420, Section 467,Section 468,Section 471, Section 472, Section 474;

Prevention Of Corruption Act, 1988 - Section 13(1), Section 13(2);

Prevention of Money-Laundering (Amendment) Act, 2005;Section 2(u),Section 2(y),Section 2(1),Section 3, Section 4,Section 19,Section 45,Section 45(1)

Hon'ble Judges/Coram: Ajay Rastogi and Bela M. Trivedi, JJ.

Equivalent Citation: 2023(246)AIC229, 2023/INSC/413, 2023(3)RCR(Criminal)617, [2023] 178SCL465(SC)

Number of Pages in the Original Judgment:10

Case Reference:

Nikesh Tarachand Shah v. Union of India (UOI) and Ors. MANU/SC/1480/2017; Pepsi Foods Ltd. and Ors. v. Special Judicial Magistrate and Ors. MANU/SC/1090/1998; State of Haryana and Ors. v. Ch. Bhajan Lal and Ors. MANU/SC/0115/1992

Case Note:

Criminal - Quashing of proceedings - Denial of - Sections 120B, 420, 467, 468, 471, 472 and 474 of Indian Penal Code, 1860, Sections 13(1)(d) and 13(2) of Prevention of Corruption Act, 1988and Sections 2(u), 2(y) and 3 of Prevention of Money Laundering Act, 2002 - FIR was registered by CBI against one person, his associates and officials of three branches of bank and certain other persons for offences under Sections 120B, 420, 467, 468, 471, 472 and 474 of Code and Section 13(2) read with 13(1)(d) of Act - It was alleged in said FIR that to defraud bank, Accused and his associates, in collusion with officials of bank had misused KYC documents of his clients/employees/family members as well as existing customers of bank -During course of investigation, it was revealed that Petitioner, his companies had received more than one hundred sixty crores defrauded funds from accounts of fictitious firms/companies - Petitioner therefore filed writ petition beforeHigh Court, seeking prayer to quash said ECIR, which stand dismissed - Hence, present appeal - Whether impugned proceedings initiated against Petitioners required to be quashed.

Facts:

An FIR came to be registered by CBI against one person, his associates and the officials of three branches of the bank and certain other persons for the offences under Sections 120B, 420, 467, 468, 471, 472 and 474 of Code and Section 13(2) read with 13(1)(d) of Act. It was alleged inter alia in the said FIR that to defraud the bank, the Accused and his associates, in collusion with the officials of bank had misused the KYC documents of his clients/employees/family members as well as the existing customers of the bank to launder the money. The CBI, filed charge-sheet before the Designated CBI Court, against accuse person and some of the officers of the bank for the said offences.Since some of the offences registered by the CBI in the said FIR were scheduled offences under the Prevention of Money Laundering Act, 2002 (PMLA), the Directorate of Enforcement (ED), initiated investigation for the offence of money laundering by registering an Enforcement Case Information Report (ECIR).During the course of investigation, it was revealed that the Petitioner had received more than sum defrauded funds from the accounts of fictitious firms/companies created and operated by accused person.The Petitioner- Anoop Bartaria therefore filed the writ petition before the High Court, seeking prayer to quash the said ECIR which stand dismissed.

Held, while dismissing the petition:

(i) Section 2(u) defines what is proceeds of crime and Section 2(y) defines what is Scheduled offence. As discernable from the record, the prosecution complaint in ECIR was lodged against the Petitioners and others under the PMLA by the ED, pursuant to the investigation carried out by the CBI and the charge-sheet filed by the CBI against for the offences under Sections 120B, 420, 467, 468, 471, 472 and 474 of Indian Penal Code and Section 13(2) read with Section 13(1)(d) of the Prevention of Corruption Act, 1988 at the Designated CBI Court. All the said offences were scheduled offences within the meaning of Section 2(y) of the said Act. The allegations against the Petitioner No. 1 as the Chairman and Managing Director of company and the Petitioner No. 2 were stated in the prosecution complaint. The Court at this juncture was not required to go into the merits of the said allegations. Suffice it to say that serious allegations of money laundering were alleged against both the Petitioners in the prosecution complaint and sufficient material particulars had been narrated in the said complaint to substantiate the said allegations, which prima facie show the direct involvement of the Petitioners in the alleged offences of money laundering as defined in Section 3 of the said PMLA. [26]

(ii) The Petitioners had also failed to make out any case of abuse of process of the court at the instance of the Respondent authorities. There being enough material to show prima facie involvement of the Petitioners in the alleged offence of money laundering, as contemplated under the PMLA the High Court had rightly dismissed the petitions filed by the Petitioners. As stated in the statement of objects and reasons of the Act, money laundering poses a serious threat not only to the financial systems of the countries but also to their integrity and sovereignty. Hence any lenient view in dealing with such offences would be a travesty of justice. [29]

ಞ

III

Enforcement Directorate, Government of India vs. Kapil Wadhawan and Ors. (27.03.2023 - SC) : MANU/SC/0329/2023

Relative Section:

Code of Criminal Procedure (CrPC) (Amendment) Act, 1978; Code of Criminal Procedure, 1973 (CrPC) - Section 56,Section 57,Section 167,Section 167(1),Section 167(2),Section 167(3),Section 173,Section 173(2), Section 173(4),Section 173(8),Section 436A,Section 468,Section 469;

Constitution of India - Article 14,Article 19,Article 21,Article 22(2),Article 51;

General Clauses Act 1897 - Section 9, Section 10;

Limitation Act, 1963; Prevention Of Money-laundering Act, 2002 - Section 3

Hon'ble Judges/Coram: K.M. Joseph, Hrishikesh Roy and B.V. Nagarathna, JJ.

Equivalent Citation: 2023 (2) KHC 663, 2023(2)RCR(Criminal)474

Number of Pages in the Original Judgment: 18
Case Reference:

Ravi Prakash Singh v. State of Bihar MANU/SC/0174/2015; M. Ravindran v. The Intelligence Officer, Directorate of Revenue Intelligence MANU/SC/0788/2020; Chaganti Satyanarayana and Ors. v. State of Andhra Pradesh MANU/SC/0165/1986; Central Bureau of Investigation, Special Investigation Cell-I, New Delhi v. Anupam J. Kulkarni MANU/SC/0335/1992; State through CBI v. Mohd. Ashraft Bhat and Ors. MANU / SC/1009/1996; State of Maharashtra v. Bharati Chandmal Varma MANU/SC/0770/2001; Aslam Babalal Desai v. State of Maharashtra MANU/SC/0001/1993; S. Kasi v. State MANU/SC/0491/2020; Rajoo alias Raj Kishore Singh v. State of Bihar (1980) 1 SCC 108; Raj Kumar v. The State of Punjab MANU/PH/0115/1979; A.R. Antulay v. R.S. Nayak and Ors. MANU/SC/0002/1988; Sundeep Kumar Bafna v. State of Maharashtra and Ors. MANU/SC/0239/2014; Rakesh Kumar Paul v. State of Assam MANU/SC/0993/2017; Union of India (UOI) v. Nirala Yadav MANU/SC/0580/2014; Uday Mohanlal Acharya v. State of Maharashtra MANU /SC/0222/2001; Sanjay Dutt v. State through C.B.I., Bombay MANU/SC/0554/1994; Bikramjit Singh v. The State of Punjab MANU/SC/0749/2020; Gautam Navlakha v. National Investigation Agency MANU/SC/0350/2021; Deepak Satyavan Kudalkar v. The State of Maharashtra MANU/MH/0843/2020; Shah Faesal and Ors. v. Union of India (UOI) and Ors. MANU/SC/0248/2020; ECON Antri Ltd. v. Rom Industries Ltd. and Ors. MANU/SC/0865/2013; Saketh India Limited and Ors. v. India Securities Limited MANU/SC/0151/1999; A.K. Gopalan v. The State of Madras MANU/SC/0012/1950; Rustom Cavasjee Cooper and Ors. v. Union of India (UOI) MANU/SC/0011/1970; Maneka Gandhi v. Union of India (UOI) and Ors. MANU /SC/0133/1978; Kesavananda Bharati Sripadagalvaru v. State of Kerala MANU/SC/0445/1973; Additional District Magistrate, Jabalpur v. Shivakant Shukla MANU/SC/0062/1976; Justice K.S. Puttaswamy and Ors. v. Union of India (UOI) and Ors. MANU/SC/1044/2017; Kharak Singh v. The State of U.P. and Ors. MANU/SC/0085/1962; State of M.P. v. Rustam and Ors. 1995 (Supp) 3 SCC 221; N. Sureya Reddy v. State of Orissa MANU/OR/0096/1984 : 1985 Crl. LJ 939 (Ori); Pragyna Singh Thakur v. State of Maharashtra MANU/SC/1101/2011 : (2011) 10 SCC 445; Batna Ram v. State of H.P. MANU/HP/0012/1980 : 1980 Crl. LJ 748 (HP); Jagdish v. State of M.P. MANU/MP/0168/1983 : 1984 Crl. LJ 79 (MP); Rakesh Kumar Paul v. State of Assam MANU/SC/0993/2017 : (2017) 15 SCC (109); Olmstead v. U.S. MANU/FENT/0008/1928 : 277 US 438 (1928); Munn v. Illinois MANU/USSC/0207/1876 : 94 U.S. 113 (1876); Francis Corallie

Mullin v. The Administrator MANU/SC/0517/1981 : 1981 AIR 746

Case Note:

Criminal - Default bail - Period of remand - Sections57, 167 and 167(2) of Code of Criminal Procedure, 1973 and Section 3 of Prevention of Money Laundering Act, 2002 - Respondents were arrested for alleged commission of offence under Section 3 of Act and were remanded on same date-It was asserted by Respondents that period of sixty days from date of remand, expired and on next day, default bail applications were presented before Court - Special Court denied default bailwith understanding that sixty days' time limit for filing complaint expired, thereby excluding date of remand - However, High Court, under impugned judgment felt that, excluding date of remand while computing sixty day period was erroneous and held that filing of Chargesheet byED, being sixty day, would entitle Respondents to default bail - Hence, present appeal - Whether date of remand was to be included or excluded, for considering claim for default bail, when computing sixty or ninety day period as contemplated in proviso (a) of Section 167(2) of Code.

Facts:

The Respondents were arrested for alleged commission of offence under Section 3 of the Prevention of Money Laundering Act, 2002 and were remanded on the same date. Through e-mail, the Enforcement Directorate (ED) claimed to file a Complaint and subsequently a physical copy thereof was tendered before the Court. The applications for enlargement of bail were moved, through e-mail and physical filing token being issued. It was asserted by the Respondents that the period of sixty days from the date of remand, expired and on the next day, the default bail applications were presented before the Court. The Special Court denied default bail with the understanding that the sixty days' time limit for filing the complaint expired. On Respondents' challenge to the rejection of their default bail applications, the High Court after analyzing the implication of the rival submissions and interpreting the statutory provisions and their applications to the facts of the case, concluded that the Special Judge incorrectly excluded the date of remand, while computing the sixty day period. Since the chargesheet by the ED was filed beyond sixty days by including the day of remand, the applicants were found to be entitled to default bail.

Held, while dismissing the appeal:

(i) Section 57 of the Code of Criminal Procedure mandates that the Accused be produced before a Magistrate within twenty four hours of arrest and under Section 167(2) the Judicial Magistrate is required to scrutinize the executive action and determine whether the rights of the Accused are not subjugated by police action. The separation of the Executive and the Judicial exercise of power, ultimately protects an individual's personal liberty which is also constitutionally protected. If the date of remand ordered by a Magistrate is ignored, then an Accused even though in custody, the same will not be counted within the sixty or ninety day period. The custody on the date of remand is distinct from the arrest of an Accused under Section 56 Code of Criminal Procedure as that is considered as a period prior to production before the Magistrate. By this logic, even if the Accused is under custody it would neither be under Section 56, nor under 167(2) of the Code of Criminal Procedure. This will lead to an apparent legal vacuum. This can however be avoided if the remand period is considered from the very day of the remand order. Furthermore, if an Accused is remanded by a Magistrate, then, the police, post judicial scrutiny, is empowered to investigate, starting on the same day, as per Section 167 Code of Criminal Procedure, irrespective of whether the police actually commence investigation on the same day. So, if the police is empowered to investigate an Accused person on the day of the remand order itself, the sixty or ninety day stipulated period, upon whose expiry, the right of default bail accrues to the Accused, should logically be calculated from that day itself. Ignoring the date of remand under Section 167 Code of Criminal Procedure in the sixty or ninety day period, would militate against the legislative intent of providing an Accused protection from being in prolonged custody, because of slothful investigation. [36]

(ii) The sixty or ninety day limit is a statutory requirement which allows the State agencies to investigate serious offences beyond the fifteen-day police custody. In case the State fails to file chargesheet or supplementary request for remand within the stipulated sixty or ninety day period, this court need to strike a balance between the rights of the individual and the restriction on those rights and prevent prolonged incarceration without legal support. The very instance, the statutory remand period ends, an indefeasible right to default bail accrues to the Accused and same needs to be guarded. The liberty of the individual is surely relative and regulated. Absolute liberty is something that cannot be conceived in a societal setting. The law therefore allows authorities to detain Accused persons and facilitate investigation. However, it is the duty of this Court to discourage prolonged incarceration. Further, the right to default bail is not extinguished by the subsequent filing of the chargesheet, and the Accused continues to have the right to default bail. [42]

(iii) Since there exists vacuum in the application and details of Section 167 Code of Criminal Procedure, we have opted for an interpretation which advances the cause of personal liberty. The Accused herein were remanded and as such, the chargesheet ought to have been filed on or before the sixtieth day. But the same was filed, which was the sixty first day of their custody. Therefore, the right to default bail accrued to the Accused persons. On that very day, the Accused filed their default bail application. The ED filed the chargesheet, later in the day. Thus, the default bail Applications were filed well before the chargesheet. In Ravindran and Bikramjit, which followed the Constitution Bench in Sanjay Duttit was rightly held that if the Accused persons avail their indefeasible right to default bail before the chargesheet/final report is filed, then such right would not stand frustrated or extinguished by any such subsequent filing. We therefore declare that the stipulated sixty or ninety day remand period under Section 167 Code of Criminal Procedure ought to be computed from the date when a Magistrate authorizes remand. If the first day of remand was excluded, the remand period, as this court notice would extend beyond the permitted sixty or ninety days' period resulting in unauthorized detention beyond the period envisaged under Section 167 Code of Criminal Procedure. In cases where the chargesheet/final report is filed on or after the sixty first/ninety first day, the Accused would be entitled to default bail. In other words, the very moment the stipulated sixty or ninety day remand period expires, an indefeasible right to default bail accrues to the Accused. [50]

(iv) The impugned order of the High Court granting default bail to the Respondents by applying the proviso (a) (ii) of Section 167(2) Code of Criminal Procedure was found to be in order. Hence, upheld the impugned judgment passed by the Single Judge of the High Court. [51]

Ratio Decidendi: Ignoring the date of remand under Section 167 Code of Criminal Procedure in the sixty or ninety day period, would militate against the legislative intent of providing an Accused protection from being in prolonged custody, because of slothful investigation.

IV

The Directorate of Enforcement vs. M. Gopal Reddy and Ors. (24.02.2023 - SC) : MANU/SC/0166/2023

Relative Section: Code of Criminal Procedure, 1973 (CrPC) - Section 438; Section 120B, Section 420, Section 471; Prevention Of Corruption Act, 1988 - Section 7, Section 13(2); Section 3, Prevention Of Money-laundering Act, 2002 - Section 4,Section 17(1), Section 45, Section 45(1), Section 50

Hon'ble Judges/Coram: M.R. Shah and C.T. Ravikumar, JJ.

Equivalent Citation: 2023(2)Crimes2(SC), 2023/INSC/163, 2023(2)J.L.J.R.25, 2023(2)MLJ(Crl)135, 2023(2)PLJR123, [2023]177SCL170(SC)

Number of Pages in the Original Judgment: 8

Case Reference:

Nikesh Tarachand Shah v. Union of India (UOI) and Ors. MANU/SC/1480/2017; P. Chidambaram v. Directorate of Enforcement MANU/SC/1209/2019; Y.S. Jagan Mohan Reddy v. Central Bureau of Investigation MANU/SC/0487/2013; The Asst. Director Enforcement Directorate v. Dr. V.C. Mohan MANU/SC/0193/2022

Case Note:

Criminal - Anticipatory bail - Cancellation of - Sections 3 and 45 of Prevention of Money Laundering Act, 2002 and Section 438 of Code of Criminal Procedure, 1973 - FIR was registered for offence of money laundering under Section 3 of Act, 2002 - Apprehending his arrest in connection with ED case for scheduled offence under Act, 2002, Respondent No. 1 approached High Court by way of anticipatory bail application under Section 438 of Code - High Court had allowed anticipatory bail application and had directed that in case of his arrest in connection with ED case he be released on bail - Hence, present appeal - Whether High Court erred in granting anticipatory bail to Respondent No. 1.

Facts:

The case was registered for the offence of money laundering under Section 3 of the Prevention of Money Laundering Act, 2002.That apprehending his arrest in connection with ED case for the scheduled offence under the Act, 2002, Respondent No. 1 approached the High Court by way of anticipatory bail application under Section 438 Code of Criminal Procedure. The High Court had allowed the anticipatory bail application and had directed that in case of his arrest in connection with ED case he be released on bail.

Held, while allowing the appeal:

(i) By the impugned judgment and order, while granting anticipatory bail the High Court had observed that the provisions of Section 45 of the Act, 2002 shall not be applicable with respect to the anticipatory bail applications/proceedings under Section 438 Code of Criminal Procedure. For which the High Court has relied upon the decision of this Court in the case of Nikesh Tarachand Shah. In the case of Dr. V.C. Mohan, this Court has specifically observed and held that it is the wrong understanding that in the case of Nikesh Tarachand Shah this Court has held that the rigour of Section 45 of the Act, 2002 shall not be applicable to the application under Section 438 Code of Criminal Procedure. In the case of Dr. V.C. Mohan in which the decision of this Court in the case of Nikesh Tarachand Shah was pressed into service, it is specifically observed by this Court that it is one thing to say that Section 45 of the Act, 2002 to offences under the ordinary law would not get attracted but once the prayer for anticipatory bail is made in connection with offence under the Act, 2002, the underlying principles and rigours of Section 45 of the Act, must get triggered-although the application is under Section 438 Code of Criminal Procedure. Therefore, the observations made by the High Court that the provisions of Section 45 of the Act, 2002 shall not be applicable in connection with an application under Section 438 Code of Criminal Procedure was just contrary to the decision in the case of Dr. V.C. Mohan and the same was on misunderstanding of the observations made in the case of Nikesh Tarachand Shah. Once the rigour under Section 45 of the Act, 2002 shall be applicable the impugned judgment and order passed by the High Court granting anticipatory bail to Respondent No. 1 was unsustainable. [5.1]

(ii) Even otherwise on merits also, the impugned judgment and order passed by the High Court granting anticipatory bail to Respondent No. 1 was erroneous and unsustainable. While granting the anticipatory bail to Respondent No. 1 the High Court had not at all considered the nature of allegations and seriousness of the offences alleged of money laundering and the offence(s) under the Act, 2002. Looking to the nature of allegations, it could be said that the same can be said to be very serious allegations of money laundering which were required to be investigated thoroughly. As per the investigating agency, they had collected some material connecting Respondent No. 1 having taken undue advantage from one person. From the impugned judgment and order passed by the High Court, it appears that the High Court had considered the matter, as if, it was dealing with the prayer for anticipatory bail in connection with the ordinary offence under IPC. [6]

Disposition: In Favour of State.

V

Rana Ayyub vs. Directorate of Enforcement through its Assistant Director (07.02.2023 - SC) : MANU/SC/0096/2023

Relative Section:

Black Money (undisclosed Foreign Income And Assets) And Imposition Of Tax Act, 2015 - Section 4;

Code of Criminal Procedure, 1973 (CrPC) - Section 2,Section 2(j),Section 177 to Section 189,Section 201, Section 219 to Section 221;

Constitution of India - Article 32; Foreign Exchange Management Act, 1999 - Section 37; Income-tax Act, 1961 - Section 133(6); Information Technology (Amendment) Act, 2008;Section 66D;

Indian Penal Code, 1860 (IPC) - Section 403, Section 406,Section 418,Section 420,Section 494, Section 495;

Prevention of Money-Laundering (Amendment) Act, 2012; Prevention Of Money-laundering Act, 2002 - Section 2(1),Section 3,Section 4,Section 5,Section 8,Section 43,Section 43(1),Section 43(2),Section 44,Section

44(1),Section 45,Section 45(1),Section 46(1),Section 50, Section 65, Section 71

Hon'ble Judges/Coram: V. Ramasubramanian and J.B. Pardiwala, JJ.

Equivalent Citation: 023(2)ACR1512, AIR2023SC875, 2023 (1) ALT (Crl.) 348 (A.P.), 2023(1) Crimes 112(SC), 2023(1)ESC177(SC), 2023/INSC/101, 2023(1)J.L.J.R.413, 2023 (1) KHC 699, 2023(1)KLT808, 2023 (1)KLT808, 2023(1)PLJR321, 2023(2)RLW1494(SC), (2023)4SCC357, [2023]177SCL1(SC), 2023(2)UC697

Number of Pages in the Original Judgment: 14

Case Reference: Kaushik Chatterjee v. State of Haryana and Ors. MANU/SC/0729/2020; Vijay Madanlal Choudhary and Ors. v. Union of India and Ors. MANU/SC/0924/2022

Case Note:

Criminal - Issuance of summons - Section 45 read with Section 44 of the Prevention of Money-laundering Act, 2002 - Challenging a summoning order issued by the Court of the Special Judge, Anti-Corruption, on a complaint lodged by the Respondent under Section 45 read with Section 44 of the Act, 2002, the Petitioner has come up with the writ petition - Whether the trial of the offence of money-laundering should follow the trial of the scheduled/predicate offence or vice versa; and whether the Court of the Special Judge, Anti-Corruption, CBI Court can be said to have exercised extra-territorial jurisdiction, even though the offence alleged, was not committed within the jurisdiction of the said Court?

Facts:

It is the case of the Petitioner that during the pandemic, she initiated crowdfunding campaign through an online crowdfunding platform named "Ketto" and ran three campaigns from April 2020 to September 2021. In connection with the same, the Mumbai Zonal Office of the Enforcement Directorate initiated an enquiry against the Petitioner under the Foreign Exchange Management Act, 1999 through an Office Order. Challenging a summoning order issued by the Court of the Special Judge, Anti-Corruption, CBI Court No. 1, Ghaziabad, on a complaint lodged by the Respondent under Sec. 45 read with Section 44 of the Prevention of Money-laundering Act, 2002, the Petitioner has come up with the writ petition under Article 32 of the Constitution of India

Held, while dismissing the petition

1. The trial of the scheduled offence should take place in the Special Court which has taken cognizance of the offence of money-laundering. The trial of the scheduled offence, insofar as the question of territorial jurisdiction is

concerned, should follow the trial of the offence of money-laundering and not vice versa. [25]

2. Since the Act contemplates the trial of the scheduled offence and the trial of the offence of money-laundering to take place only before the Special Court constituted under Section 43(1), a doubt is prone to arise as to whether all the offences are to be tried together. This doubt is sought to be removed by Explanation (i) to Section 44(1). Explanation (i) clarifies that the trial of both sets of offences by the same Court shall not be construed as joint trial. [26]

3. A careful dissection of Clauses (a) and (c) of Sub-section (1) of Section 44 shows that they confer primacy upon the Special Court constituted Under Section 43(1) of the PMLA. These two clauses contain two Rules, namely, (i) that the offence punishable under the PMLA as well as a scheduled offence connected to the same shall be triable by the Special Court constituted for the area in which the offence of money-laundering has been committed; and (ii) that if cognizance has been taken by one Court, in respect of the scheduled offence and cognizance has been taken in respect of the offence of money-laundering by the Special Court, the Court trying the scheduled offence shall commit it to the Special Court trying the offence of money-laundering. [27]

4. It is only because of the Special Court constituted under Section 43(1) being conferred primacy that Section 44(1) begins with the words "notwithstanding anything contained in the Code of Criminal Procedure, 1973 (CrPC)". Though the PMLA contains a non-obstante Clause in relation to the Code of Criminal Procedure, both in Section 44(1) and in Section 45(1), there are two other provisions where the Code of Criminal Procedure is specifically declared to apply to the proceedings before a Special Court. Section 46(1) specifically makes the provisions of the CrPC applicable to proceedings before a Special Court. Similarly, Section 65 of the PMLA makes the provisions of CrPC apply to arrest, search and seizure, attachment, confiscation, investigation, prosecution and all other proceedings under the Act. [28]

5. Therefore, it is clear that the provisions of the CrPC are applicable to all proceedings under the Act including proceedings before the Special Court, except to the extent they are specifically excluded. Hence, Section 71 of the PMLA providing an overriding effect, has to be construed in tune with Section 46(1) and Section 65. [29]

6. The only contingency that could not have been provided in the above provisions of the CrPC, is perhaps where the offence of money-laundering is committed. This is why Section 44(1) begins with a non-obstante clause. The whole picture is thus complete with a combined reading of Section 44 of the PMLA and the provisions of Sections 177 to 184 of the Code of Criminal Procedure. [35]

7. In view of the specific mandate of Clauses (a) and (c) of Sub-section (1) of Section 44, it is the Special Court constituted under the PMLA that would have jurisdiction to try even the scheduled offence. Even if the scheduled offence is taken cognizance of by any other Court, that Court shall commit the same, on an application by the concerned authority, to the Special Court which has taken cognizance of the offence of money-laundering. [36]

8. The involvement of a person in any one or more of certain processes or activities connected with the proceeds of crime, constitutes the offence of money-laundering. These processes or activities include, (i) concealment; (ii) possession; (iii) acquisition; (iv) use; (v) projecting as untainted property; or (vi) claiming as untainted property. [38]

9. Therefore, the issue of territorial jurisdiction cannot be decided in a writ petition, especially when there is a serious factual dispute about the place/places of commission of the offence. Hence, this question should be raised by the Petitioner before the Special Court, since an answer to the same would depend upon evidence as to the places where any one or more of the processes or activities mentioned in Section 3 were carried out. Therefore, giving liberty to the Petitioner to raise the issue of territorial jurisdiction before the Trial Court, this writ petition is dismissed. [46]

Ratio Decidendi: Issue of territorial jurisdiction cannot be decided in a writ petition, especially when there is a serious factual dispute about the place/places of commission of the offence

Disposition: In Favour of Accused.

VI

Bikram Chatterji and Ors. vs. Union of India (UOI) and Ors. (07.11.2022 - SC) : MANU/ SC/1484/2022

Relative Section: Prevention Of Money-laundering Act, 2002 -Section 5(1);Constitution of India – Art.226

Hon'ble Judges/Coram: U.U. Lalit, C.J.I., Ajay Rastogi and Bela M. Trivedi, JJ.

Equivalent Citation: : 2022/INSC/1180

Number of Pages in the Original Judgment: 29

Case Reference: Bikram Chatterji and Ors. v. Union of India and Ors. MANU/SC/0947/2019; Central Inland Water Transport Corporation Limited and Anr. v. Brojo Nath Ganguly and Anr. MANU/SC/0439/1986 : (1986) S SCC 156; Jagdish Mandal v. State of Orissa MANU/SC/0090/2007 : (2007) 14 SCC 531

Case Note:

Property -Recall of orders - Applications has been filed by Greater Noida Authority seeking recall of the orders dated 10.06.2020, 19.08.2020 and 25.08.2020 in so far as they related to interest charged by the Applicant on all projects other than the Amrapali Project - Whether Present Court erred in granting relief to projects other than Amrapali Group of Companies vide its orders? Facts: Instant applications have been preferred on behalf of the Greater Noida Authority and NOIDA Authority seeking recall of the orders dated 10.06.2020, 19.08.2020 and 25.08.2020 passed by this Court. It is submitted that, the orders provide no jurisprudential basis for overriding contractual interest and that too only in relation to the Applicant. There are multifarious contracts entered into by parties in relation to supplies of goods and services. All these contracts contain interest provisions. The levy of compound interest, on a contractual basis, is not just well established in India but is well established internationally. The charging of interest under a contract is a matter of negotiation between the parties and once a contract is entered into, the sanctity of the contract cannot be forsaken in this manner without there being any supervening illegality being established in relation to any term the contract. Held, while allowing the applications 1. In these proceedings present Courtis principally concerned with the plight of flat holders of Amrapali Group of Companies. In order to see that the projects do not remain stalled and the investment made by all the flat buyers comes out of cloud of uncertainty, certain measures were adopted by this Court in its order dated 23.07.2019. Those measures contemplated restriction on the Noida and Greater Noida Authorities to resume the properties in question, as well as, cancellation of lease deed granted in favour of Amrapali Group of Companies and vesting all the rights in favour of the Court Receiver and NBCC was appointed to complete various projects. These directions were passed in the peculiar facts and circumstances in Amrapali Projects. It was in light of these directions that one of the issues which came up for consideration before the Court related to reduction in rate of interest. The dues payable to Noida or Greater Noida in respect of projects of Amrapali Group of Companies would otherwise have been liable to pay along with interest at certain rates. Since that would have put additional burden on the entire project, it was deemed appropriate to consider reduction in rate of interest. [14]

2. At that juncture, an application filed on behalf of ACE group of companies was listed for the first time on 27.05.2020 by which time the note prepared by the learned Court Receiver seeking reduction in rate of interest for Amrapali Group of Companies was taken up on 25.05.2020 and the order was reserved. The order dated 27.05.2020, as extracted hereinabove noted the fact that similar matter was under consideration and therefore reserved order in that matter. The record indicates, no reply was filed by the concerned authorities nor were they may aware of the impact of such application preferred by ACE Group of Companies. [15]

3. The order dated 10.06.2020 did consider the case projected by ACE group of companies in its application dated 27.05.2020 but as indicated earlier, there was no response on behalf of the concerned authorities. It must be noted that this Court in the present matter was not in any way concerned with the facts and circumstances pertaining to any of the flat buyers in projects of ACE Group of Companies. No grievance was raised by anybody that the individual flat buyers were put to prejudice as a result of rate of interest charged on the amounts due. What was under consideration before the court was the peculiar fact situation pertaining to Amrapali Group of Companies. Neither was there any general petition on behalf of any or all builders of Noida or Greater Noida in a manner known to law nor was the scope of the matter vide enough to consider any such plea advanced on behalf of ACE Group of Companies. [16]

4. Around this time a decision was taken by the State Government on 09.06.2020 giving reduction in interest rates generally to all builders pertaining to all projects. However, this Court was not aware of the order dated 09.06.2020 when the order was pronounced on 10.06.2020 in the matter reserved earlier. It is true that though it was completely beyond the scope of instant matters to consider the cases of other builders, this Court did to consider the case of builders such as ACE group of companies and the matter was dealt with in its order dated 10.06.2020. However, at that juncture it was not known to this Court that huge amount running into more than Rs. 3000 - 4000 crores for Noida and Greater Noida Authorities, would be in issue. [17]

5. As a result of the orders passed by this Court the builders are now asking for adjustment of whatever they had paid earlier and in certain cases they are even demanding refund of the amount paid in excess. In every case, the concerned builder had opted for allocation of plot on the basis of brochure which had clearly indicated the rate of interest. The allotment letter and consequential lease deed carried the same intent. Thus, every builder was well aware and had entered into transaction with Noida and Greater Noida Authorities with open eyes. Whatever was the impact on account of that rate of interest must have been subsumed in the price which was arrived at and had to be paid by every flat holder. [18]

6. In cases where contractual terms were sought to be invalidated this Court has repeatedly refrained from entering into such issues. [19]

7. If even in normal circumstances, the interference with contractual terms is not easily to be taken resort to, it does not stand to reason that in a matter with which this Court was not even concerned, the benefit could be extended to the entire body of builders of Noida and Greater Noida. Reference made to a number of stalled projects including some of the projects of the builders who are presently before us, cannot be taken as an indication that the benefits which were to be extended to the flat buyers from Amrapali Group of Companies must also be extended to the flat buyers to the other projects from Noida or Greater Noida. [20]

8. Some of the orders, namely the order pertaining to IA No. 74824 of 2020 allowing Supertech Group of Companies to withdraw their application as well as order dated 07.09.2020 in Contempt Petition Nos. 52525, 52526, 52527 of 2020 stating that no contempt was made out, are an indication that this Court was not concerned that the matter pertaining to projects other than Amrapali Group of Companies. [21]

9. The objections that the proper jurisdiction to be exercised would be jurisdiction in review, is purely technical. The matter was dealt with by the Bench dealing with questions relating to Amrapali Group of Companies. The circumstances delineated also show that a completely different matter came to be dealt with by the Bench principally concerned with matters of Amrapali Group of Company. No adequate notice was given to the concerned Authorities and the exact impact of the decisions was also not made known to the Court when these orders were passed. Present Court have therefore have no hesitation in rejecting all these technical submissions. [22]

10. Present Court erred in granting relief to projects other than Amrapali Group of Companies vide its orders dated 10.06.2020, 19.08.2020 and 25.08.2020. [23]

11. Consequently, the instant applications are allowed and the orders are recalled, as prayed. The Noida and Greater Noida Authorities are directed to calculate the amount due in respect of builders other than Amrapali Group of Companies after taking into consideration the effect of the order dated 09.06.2020 issued by the State Government. [24]

Facts: Certain facts which have led to the filing of the instant applications must be adverted to.

A. In Writ Petition (C) No. 940 of 2017 which raises grievances on behalf of the purchasers of flats in projects promoted by the Amrapali Group of Companies, this Court has been passing various directions including appointment of Forensic Auditors. When the matter was listed on 22.05.2020, in response to a suggestion made by the learned Receiver in his Note, the applicants were called upon to obtain instructions with regard to interest to be charged and levied on the outstanding premium on account of defaults committed by Amrapali Group of Companies. The matter was then adjourned to 27.05.2020.

Held, while allowing the appeal

35. There are two divergent views which are emanating from the record. According to the forensic auditors, the liability of Mr. Prem Mishra is to the tune of Rs. 10.26 crores and also in the additional sum of Rs. 2.31 crores; whereas, according to the ED, the extent of funds siphoned off by Mr. Prem Mishra were to the tune of Rs. 4,79,76,180 only. But at the root of the entire controversy is the question whether Mr. Prem Mishra has any claim or title with respect to the property which is subject matter of attachment. The documents on which reliance has been placed in I.A. Nos. 8259 of 2019 and 74385 of 2020 are not registered documents nor have these I. As. been finally disposed of. Going by the tenor of I.A. No. 8259 of 2019, it is directed against the proceedings dated 11.12.2018, where the matter was not gone into by the DRT-III, New Delhi because of pendency of proceedings in this Court. There is thus no concrete and final determination with regard to the rights of Mr. Prem Mishra to the property which was subject matter of arrangements between the parties. Even at this stage, going by the prima facie view, at least Rs. 21 crores were invested by Amrapali Group of Companies for purchase of these lands. By any standard, even without expressing any opinion on merits of the matter, the bulk of the investment has come from Amrapali Group of Companies towards purchase of these properties. Merely because the extent of money which was siphoned off has been put at the level of Rs. 4.79 crores would not mean that lands beyond this value ought to be released in favour of Mr. Prem Mishra. His entitlement is yet to be pronounced upon.

36. In the circumstances, the prayer made by Mr. Prem Mishra for releasing attachment of all the assets in question, cannot be granted at this stage. In essence, the matter has to be considered along with I.A. Nos. 8259 of 2019 and 74385 of 2020. We, therefore, reject the prayer for release of attachment as mentioned above and direct that these two Interlocutory

Applications be listed and considered at an early date.

VII

J. Sekar vs. Directorate of Enforcement (05.05.2022 - SC) : MANU /SC/0596/ 2022

Relative Section:

Code of Criminal Procedure, 1973 (CrPC) - Section 161, Section 173 (2),Section 300, Section 482;

Constitution of India - Article 20(2); Indian Penal Code, 1860 (IPC) - Section 120B, Section 409, Section 420; Prevention Of Corruption Act, 1988 - Section 13(1),Section 13(2);Section 2(1),Section 3,Section 4,Section 5(1), Section 5(5),Section 8(1),Section 8(5),Section 44(1)

Hon'ble Judges/Coram: Vineet Saran and J.K. Maheshwari, JJ.

Equivalent Citation: 22(235)AIC235, 2022 (120) ACC 700, 2022 (2) ALT (Crl.) 204 (A.P.), 2022 (3) Bom CR(Cri)131, 2022(2)Crimes285(SC), 2022/INSC/ 519, 2022(5)JKJ309[SC], 2022(3)KLJ135, 2022 (2) RCR (Criminal)976, (2022)7SCC370, [2022]172SCL555(SC), [2022]3SCR698

Number of Pages in the Original Judgment: 11

Case Reference: Radheshyam Kejriwal v. State of West Bengal and Ors. MANU/SC/0134/2011; Ashoo Surendranath Tewari v. The Deputy Superintendent of Police, EOW, CBI and Ors. MANU/SC/0777/2020

Case Note:

Criminal - Quashing of proceedings - Section 120-B read with Section 409, 420 of Indian Penal Code, 1860 (IPC) - Section 13(2), read with Section 13(1)(c) and 13(1)(d) of the Prevention of Corruption Act, 1988 (PC Act) - Section 482 of the Code of Criminal Procedure, 1973 (CrPC) - Sections 3 and 4 of the Prevention of Money Laundering Act, 2002 (PMLA) - High Court vide impugned judgment rejected the petition seeking quashing of proceedings - Hence the present appeal - Whether impugned judgment in view of the facts and circumstances of the case sustainable or liable to be set aside?

Facts:

The present appeal was filed against the impugned judgment dismissing the petition filed for quashing of proceedings. The impugned judgment rejected Appellant's contention that FIR with respect to Schedule offence was closed for want of evidence and in absence of connected evidence with a crime of Schedule offence, prosecution for offences under Sections 3 & 4 of the PMLAunsustainable. It was also held that the offence of money laundering is independent of the Schedule offence because PMLA deals with the process or activity with respect to the proceeds of crime including concealment, possession, acquisition or use. However in the light of the explanation of Section 44(1) of PMLA, the argument of the Appellant was repelled. Appellant, Managing Partner of a partnership firm engaged in sand mining was subjected tocase registered by CBI for offences under Sections 120-B r/w 409, 420 of IPC and Section 13(2), r/w 13(1)(c) and 13(1)(d) of the PC Act against the Appellant and two others.

Held, while allowing the Appeal:

For proceeds of crime, as defined under Section 2(1)(u) of PMLA, the property seized would be relevant and its possession with recovery and claim thereto must be innocent. In the present case, the Schedule offence has not been made out because of lack of evidence. The Adjudicating Authority, at the time of refusing to continue the order of attachment under PMLA, was of the opinion that the record regarding banks and its officials who may be involved, is not on record. Therefore, for lack of identity of the source of collected money, it could not be reasonably believed by the Deputy Director (ED) that the unaccounted money is connected with the commission of offence under PMLA. Even in cases of PMLA, the Court cannot proceed on the basis of preponderance of probabilities. On perusal of the statement of Objects and Reasons specified in PMLA, it is the stringent law brought by Parliament to check money laundering. Thus, the allegation must be proved beyond reasonable doubt in the Court. Even otherwise, it is incumbent upon the Court to look into the allegation and the material collected in support thereto and to find out whether the prima facie offence is made out. Unless the allegations are substantiated by the authorities and proved against a person in the court of law, the person is innocent. [19]

Looking to the facts as discussed hereinabove and the ratio of the judgments of this Court in RadheshyamKejriwal (supra) and AshooSurendranathTewari (supra), the chance to prove the allegations even for the purpose of provisions of PMLA in the Court are bleak. Therefore, till the allegations are proved, the Appellant would be innocent. The High Court by the impugned order has recorded the finding without due consideration of the letter of the I.T. Department and other material in right perspective. Therefore, these findings of the High Court cannot be sustained.[20]

Accordingly, appeal is allowed. [21]

Disposition: In Favour of Accused.

VIII

Opto Circuit India Ltd. vs. Axis Bank and Ors. (03.02.2021 - SC) : MANU/SC/0049/2021

Relative Section:

Code of Criminal Procedure, 1973 (CrPC) - Section 102, Section 102(3);120(B),Section 420,Section 468, Section 471;Section 13(1),Section 13(2);Section 2(v),Section 2(w),Section 2(1),Section 3,Section 4,Section 8(5),Section 8(7),Section 16,Section 17,Section 17(1),Section 17(1A),Section 17(2),Section 17(4)Section 58B, Section 60(2A),Section 71

Hon'ble Judges/Coram: S.A. Bobde, C.J.I., A.S. Bopanna and V. Ramasubramanian, JJ

Equivalent Citation:

2021(219)AIC120, AIR2021SC753, 2021(2) AKR 39, 2021 (115) ACC 735, 2021 (2) ALT (Crl.) 247 (A.P.), III(2021)BC283(SC), 2021(2)BLJ131, 2021(1)BomCR(Cri)666, 2021CriLJ1636, 2021(1)Crimes160(SC), 2021(2)CTC210, 2021/INSC/56, 2021(3)J.L.J.R.55, 2021(1)JKJ42[SC], 2021(1)N.C.C.599, 2021(3)PLJR47, 2021(1)RCR(Criminal)856, (2021)6SCC707, 2021 (1) SCJ 732, [2021]165SCL703(SC), [2021]2SCR81

Number of Pages in the Original Judgment: 9

Case Reference: Mohinder Singh Gill and Ors. v. The Chief Election Commissioner, New Delhi and Ors. MANU/SC/0209/1977; Chandra Kishore

Jha v. Mahavir Prasad and Ors. MANU/SC/0594/1999

Case Note:

Criminal - Freezing of account - Quashing of - Action initiated by Central Bureau of Investigation (CBI) for alleged predicate offence - Enforcement Directorate in order to track money trail relating to predicate offence and prevent layering of same had initiated proceedings under PMLA - In said process the Deputy Director, Directorate of Enforcement through communication addressed to Anti Money-Laundering Officer of Respondents No. 1 to 3 Banks instructed them that accounts maintained by Appellant company be debit freezed/stop operations - Appellant claiming to be aggrieved filed writ petition before High Court to quash communication issued for debit freezing account - High Court upheld action - Hence, present appeal - Whether impugned order of freezing of account was in consonance with law.

Facts:

The action initiated by the Central Bureau of Investigation for the alleged predicate offence and the instant proceedings is a fall out of the same. It was in that background the Enforcement Directorate in order to track the money trail relating to the predicate offence and prevent layering of the same has initiated the proceedings under the PMLA. In the said process the Deputy Director, Directorate of Enforcement through the communication addressed to the Anti Money-Laundering Officer of Respondents No. 1 to 3 Banks instructed them that the accounts maintained by the Appellant company be debit freezed/stop operations until further orders, with immediate effect. It was in that light the Appellant claiming to be aggrieved filed writ petition before the High Court seeking for issue of an appropriate writ to quash the communication issued for debit freezing the account. The High Court considered the matter in detail and has taken into consideration the object with which the PMLA was enacted and the validity of the Act being considered by the High Court in the decisions referred to in the course of the order. The permissibility and scope of parallel proceedings under Section 3 and 4 of PMLA was adverted to in detail and upheld the action.

Held, while allowing the appeal:

(i) The scheme of the PMLA is well intended. While it seeks to achieve the object of preventing money laundering and bring to book the offenders, it also safeguards the rights of the persons who would be proceeded against under the Act by ensuring fairness in procedure. Hence a procedure, including timeline is provided so as to ensure that power is exercised for the purpose to which the officer is vested with such power and the Adjudicating Authority is also kept in the loop. In the instant case, the procedure contemplated under Section 17 of PMLA to which reference was made above has not been followed by the Officer Authorised. Except issuing the impugned communication to AML Officer to seek freezing, no other procedure contemplated in law was followed. In fact, the impugned communication did not even refer to the belief of the Authorised Officer even if the same was recorded separately. It only states that the Officer is investigating the case and seeks for relevant documents, but in the tabular column abruptly states that the accounts have to be debit freezed/stop operations. It certainly is not the requirement that the communication addressed to the Bank itself should contain all the details. But what is necessary is an order in the file recording the belief as provided under Section 17(1) of PMLA before the communication was issued and thereafter the requirement of Section 17(2) of PMLA after the freezing was made was complied. There was no other material placed before the Court to indicate compliance of Section 17 of PMLA, more particularly recording the belief of commission of the act of money laundering and placing it before the Adjudicating Authority or for filing application after securing the freezing of the account to be made. In that view, the freezing or the continuation thereof was without due compliance of the legal requirement and, therefore, not sustainable. [11]

(ii) The Respondent made a subtle attempt to contend that the power of seizure was available under Section 102 of the Code of Criminal Procedure, which had been exercised and as such the freezing of the account would remain valid. This court were unable to appreciate and accept such contention for more than one reason. Firstly, as noted, it had been the contention of Respondent No. 4 that PMLA was a standalone enactment. If that be so and when such enactment contains a provision for seizure which includes freezing, the power available therein was to be exercised and the procedure contemplated therein is to be complied. Secondly, when the power was available under the special enactment, the question of resorting to the power under the general law did not arise. Thirdly, the power under Section 102 Code of Criminal Procedure was to the Police Officer during the course of investigation and the scheme of the provision was different from the scheme under PMLA. Further, even Sub-section (3) to Section 102 Code of Criminal Procedure requires that the Police Officer shall forthwith report the seizure to the Magistrate having jurisdiction, the compliance of which is also not shown if the said provision was in fact invoked. That apart, the impugned communication did not refer to the power being exercised under the Code of Criminal Procedure. [12]

(iii) Therefore, the communication was quashed and direct that the Respondents shall defreeze the accounts and honour payments advised by the Appellant towards statutory dues. [17]

Disposition: Appeal Partly Allowed.

IX

P. Chidambaram vs. Directorate of Enforcement (04.12.2019 - SC) : MANU/SC/1670/2019

Relative Section:

Code of Criminal Procedure, 1973 (CrPC) - Section 267,Section 437,Section 438,Section 439;

Indian Penal Code, 1860 (IPC) - Section 120B, Section 420; Prevention of Corruption Act - Section 8, Prevention of Corruption Act - Section 13(1), Prevention of Corruption Act - Section 13(2); Prevention of Money-laundering Act, 2002 - Section 3, Prevention Of Money-laundering Act, 2002 - Section 4

Hon'ble Judges/Coram: R. Banumathi, A.S. Bopanna and Hrishikesh Roy, JJ

Equivalent Citation: 2020(211)AIC78, AIR2020SC1699, 2019(3)ALT(Crl.)529(A.P.), 2020(1)BLJ200,

2019 (4)Crimes253(SC), 265(2019)DLT1, 2019/INSC/1317, 2020(1)J.L.J.R.88, 2020-1-LW(Crl)580,

2020(1)MLJ(Crl)28, 2020(1)PLJR170,2019(16)SCALE870, (2020)13SCC791, 2020(2)SCJ112, [2020]157SCL649 (SC), [2019]14SCR450

Number of Pages in the Original Judgment: 14

Case Reference:

Rohit Tandon v. The Enforcement Directorate MANU/SC/1403/2017; Seniors Fraud Investigation Office v. Nittin Johari and Anr. MANU/SC/1246/2019; Sanjay Chandra v. CBI MANU/SC/1375/2011; Prahlad Singh Bhati v. N.C.T. Delhi & Anr. MANU/SC/0193/2001; The State of Bihar and Ors. v. Amit Kumar MANU/SC/0515/2017; Nimmagadda Prasad v. Central Bureau of Investigation MANU/SC/0485/2013; Y.S. Jagan Mohan Reddy v. Central Bureau of Investigation MANU/SC/0487/2013; State of Gujarat v. Mohanlal Jitamalji Porwal and Anr. MANU/SC/0288/1987; Shri Gurbaksh Singh Sibbia and Ors. v. State of Punjab MANU/SC/0215/1980; Nagendra Nath Chakrabarthi v. King-Emperor MANU/WB/0119/1923; K.N. Joglekar v. Emperor MANU/UP/0060/1931; Emperor v. H.L. Hutchinson MANU/UP/0014/1931; P. Chidambaram v. CBI Crl. Appeal No. 1603/2019; CBI v. Ramendu Chattopadhyay Crl. Appeal No. 1711 of 2019

Case Note:

Criminal - Bail - Grant of - Section 439 of Code of Criminal Procedure, 1973; Section 3 and 4 of Prevention of Money Laundering Act, 2002 - Respondent registered case against Appellant under Section 3 of Act punishable under Section 4 of Act - Subsequently, Appellant was arrested and Trial Court remanded Appellant to custody of Respondent - After his arrest, Appellant moved regular bail application before High Court under Section 439 of Code - High Court concluded that prima facie, allegations were serious in nature and Appellant had played key and active role in present case - High Court dismissed bail application filed by Appellant - Hence, present appeal - Whether Appellant is entitled to bail.

Facts:

The Respondent Directorate of Enforcement registered a case against Appellant-Accused under Section 3 of Prevention of Money Laundering Act, 2002 punishable under Section 4 of the said Act with allegations that one company sought approval of Foreign Investment Promotion Board for permission to issue by way of preferential allotment, certain equity and convertible, non-cumulative, redeemable preference shares for engaging in the business of creating, operating, managing and broadcasting of bouquet of television channels. This proposal was favourably considered and approved by the Appellant. Subsequently, the Appellant was arrested and the Trial Court remanded the Appellant to the custody of the Respondent. After his arrest, the Appellant moved a regular bail application before the High Court under Section 439 of Code of Criminal Procedure, 1973. The High Court concluded that prima facie, allegations are serious in nature and the Appellant had played key and active role in the present case. On the basis of these observations, the High Court dismissed the bail application.

Held, while allowing the appeal:

(i) This Court was not very much inclined to open the sealed cover although the materials in sealed cover was received from the Respondent. However, since the Single Judge of the High Court had perused the documents in sealed cover and arrived at certain conclusion and since that order was under challenge, it had become imperative to also open the sealed cover and peruse the contents so as to satisfy ourselves to that extent. On perusal this Court had taken note that the statements of persons concerned had been recorded and the details collected have been collated. The recording of statements and the collation of material was in the nature of allegation against one of the Co-Accused for opening shell companies and also purchasing benami properties in the name of relatives at various places in different countries. Except for recording the same, this court did not wish to advert to the documents any further since ultimately, these were allegations which would have to be established in the trial wherein the Accused/Co-Accused would have the opportunity of putting forth their case, if any, and an ultimate conclusion would be reached. Hence, the finding recorded by the Judge of the High Court based on the material in sealed cover was not justified. [24]

(ii) While considering the bail application of the Appellant what was to be taken note was that, at a stage when the Appellant was before this Court in an application seeking for interim protection/anticipatory bail, this Court while considering the matter in Criminal Appeal had in that regard held that in a matter of present nature wherein grave economic offence was alleged, custodial interrogation as contended would be necessary and in that circumstance the anticipatory bail was rejected. Subsequently the Appellant had been taken into custody and had been interrogated and for the said purpose the Appellant was available in custody in this case. It was, however, contended on behalf of the Respondent that the witnesses will have to be confronted and as such custody was required for that purpose. The Appellant had not been named as one of the Accused in the ECIR but the allegation while being made against the Co-Accused it was indicated the

Appellant who was the Finance Minister at that point, had aided the illegal transactions since one of the Co-Accused was the son of the Appellant. In this context even if the statements on record and materials gathered were taken note, the complicity of the Appellant would have to be established in the trial and if convicted, the Appellant would undergo sentence. For the present, as taken note the anticipatory bail had been declined earlier and the Appellant was available for custodial interrogation for more than forty five days. In addition to the custodial interrogation if further investigation was to be made, the Appellant would be bound to participate in such investigation as is required by the Respondent. Further it was noticed that one of the Co-Accused had been granted bail by the High Court while the other Co-Accused was enjoying interim protection from arrest. The Appellant was aged about seventy four years and as noted by the High Court itself in its order, the Appellant had already suffered two bouts of illness during incarceration and was put on antibiotics and had been advised to take steroids of maximum strength. In that circumstance, the availability of the Appellant for further investigation, interrogation and facing trial was not jeopardized and he was already held to be not a flight risk and there was no possibility of tampering the evidence or influencing/intimidating the witnesses. Taking these and all other facts and circumstances including the duration of custody into consideration the Appellant was entitled to be granted bail. It was made clear that the observations contained touching upon the merits either in the order of the High Court or in this order shall not be construed as an opinion expressed on merits and all contentions were left open to be considered during the course of trial. [25]

Disposition: In Favour of Accused.

X

P. Chidambaram vs. Directorate of Enforcement (05.09.2019 - SC) : MANU/SC/1209/2019

Relative Section:

Code of Criminal Procedure, 1973 (CrPC) - Section 161,Section 172,Section 172(2),Section

172(3), Section 173, Section 173(8),Section 190,Section 438,Section 482,Section 491;

Constitution of India - Article 14, Article 20, Article 20(1),Article 20(3),Article 21;

Evidence Act - Section 145,Section 161; Explosives Substances Act, 1908;

Indian Penal Code, 1860 (IPC) - Section 26, 1860 (IPC) - Section 420;

Narcotic Drugs and Psychotropic Substances Act, 1985;

Prevention of Corruption (Amendment) Act, 2008; Prevention of Corruption (Amendment) Act, 2009; Prevention of Corruption (Amendment) Act, 2013; Prevention of Corruption (Amendment) Act, 2018; Prevention Of Corruption Act, 1988 - Section 8, Section 13,Section 13(1), Section 13(2);

Prevention Of Money-laundering (forms And The Manner Of Forwarding A Copy Of Order Of Arrest Of A Person Along With The Material To The Adjudicating Authority And Its Period Of Retention) Rules, 2005 - Rule 3; Prevention of Money-Laundering (Forms, Search and Seizure or Freezing and the Manner of Forwarding the Reasons and Material to the Adjudicating Authority, Impounding and Custody of Records and the period of Retention) Rules, 2005; Prevention Of Money-laundering (manner Of Forwarding A Copy Of The Order Of Provisional Attachment Of Property Along With The Material, And Copy Of Material In Respect Of Survey, To The Adjudicating Authority And Its Period Of Retention) Rules, 2005 - Rule 3;

Prevention Of Money-laundering Act, 2002 -Section 2(1),Section 3,Section 4,Section 5,Section 5(2), Section 17,Section 19,Section 19(1),Section 19(3),Section 45,Section 45(1),Section 55,Section 56,Section 57,Section 58, Section 59,Section 60,Section 61,Section 65,Section 71,Section 73

Hon'ble Judges/Coram: R. Banumathi and A.S. Bopanna, JJ.

Equivalent Citation: AIR2019SC4198, 2019 (3) ALT (Crl.) 188 (A.P.), 2019(4)BomCR(Cri)809, 2019 CriLJ4754, 2019(3)Crimes410(SC), 2019/INSC/ 1010, 2019(4)J.L.J.R.127, 2020-1-LW(Crl)542, 2019 (4) MLJ (Crl)188, 2019(3)N.C.C.384, 2019(4)PLJR19, 2019(4)RCR(Criminal)875, 2019(12)SCALE94, (2019)9SCC24, 2020 (1) SCJ 752, [2019]156SCL104(SC), [2019]12SCR172

Number of Pages in the Original Judgment: 28

Case Reference:

Shri Gurbaksh Singh Sibbia and Ors. v. State of Punjab MANU/SC/0215/ 1980; Additional District Magistrate, Jabalpur v. Shivakant Shukla MANU/ SC/0062/1976; Rao Shiv Bahadur Singh and Anr. v. The State of Vindhya Pradesh MANU/SC/0081/1953; Santosh v. The State of Maharashtra MANU/ SC/1313/2017; Romila Thapar and Ors. v. Union of India (UOI) and Ors. MANU/SC/1098/2018; Jai Prakash Singh v. State of Bihar and Anr. etc. MANU/SC/0224/2012; Director of Enforcement and another v. P.V. Prabhakar Rao MANU/SC/0958/1997; Nikesh Tarachand Shah v. Union of India (UOI) and Ors. MANU/SC/1480/2017; Balakram v. State of Uttarakhand and Ors. MANU/SC/0483/2017; Sidharth etc. etc. v. State of Bihar MANU/SC/0949/2005; Naresh Kumar Yadav v. Ravindra Kumar and Ors. MANU/SC/8067/2007; Malkiat Singh and Ors. v. State of Punjab MANU/SC/0622/1991; R.K. Krishna Kumar v. State of Assam and Ors. MANU/SC/0858/1998; Mukund Lal v. Union of India (UOI) and Anr. MANU/ SC/0322/1988; Emperor v. Khwaja Nazir Ahmad MANU/PR/0007/1944; Abhinandan Jha and Ors. v. Dinesh Mishra MANU/SC/0054/1967; State of

Bihar and Anr. v. J.A.C. Saldanha and Ors. MANU/SC/0253/1979; Mian Saleh Mohammad Shah v. Sayyad Zawar Hussain Shah and Anr. MANU/PR/0034/1943; Dukhishyam Benupani, Asstt. Director, Enforcement Directorate (FERA) v. Arun Kumar Bajoria MANU/SC/0872/1998; M.C. Abraham and Anr., v. State of Maharashtra and Ors. MANU/SC/1190/2002; Dr. Subramanian Swamy v. Director, Central Bureau of Investigation and Anr. MANU/SC/0417/2014; Divine Retreat Centre v. State of Kerala and Ors. MANU/SC/1150/2008; State of M.P. and Anr. v. Ram Kishna Balothia and Anr. MANU/SC/0239/1995; State Rep. by the C.B.I. v. Anil Sharma MANU/SC/0947/1997; Sudhir and Ors. v. The State of Maharashtra and Ors. MANU/SC/1095/2015; Adri Dharan Das v. State of West Bengal MANU/SC/0120/2005; Siddharam Satlingappa Mhetre v. State of Maharashtra and Ors. MANU/SC/1021/2010; D.K. Ganesh Babu v. P.T. Manokaran and Ors. MANU/SC/1086/2007; State of Maharashtra and Anr. v. Mohd. Sajid Husain Mohd. S. Husain etc. MANU/SC/8008/2007; Union of India (UOI) v. Padam Narain Aggarwal etc. MANU/SC/4230/2008; Directorate of Enforcement v. Ashok Kumar Jain MANU/SC/0007/1998; State of Gujarat v. Mohanlal Jitamalji Porwal and Anr. MANU/SC/0288/1987; Y.S. Jagan Mohan Reddy v. Central Bureau of Investigation MANU/SC/0487/2013; Enforcement Officer, Ted, Bombay v. Bher Chand Tikaji Bora and Anr. MANU/SC/0970/1999; State of Bihar and Anr. v. P.P. Sharma, IAS and Anr. MANU/SC/0542/1992 : 1992 Supp. (1) 222; Assistant Director, Directorate of Enforcement v. Hassan Ali Khan MANU/SC/0446/2011 : (2011) 12 SCC 684

Case Note:

Criminal - Anticipatory bail - Denial of - Sections 120B and 420 of Code of Criminal Procedure, 1973, Section 8 and Section 13(2) read with Section 13(1)(d) of Prevention of Corruption Act, 1988 and Sections 3 and 4 of Prevention of Money-Laundering Act, 2002 - CBI registered FIR under Section 120B of Code read with Section 420 of Code, Section 8 and Section 13(2) read with Section 13(1)(d) of Act against Accused for alleged irregularities in Foreign Investment Promotion Board (FIPB) clearance given to company for receiving foreign investment - Enforcement Directorate also registered case against accused persons for allegedly committing offence punishable under Sections 3 and 4 of Act - Appellant moved High Court seeking anticipatory bail in both cases - High Court rejected Appellant's plea for anticipatory bail in both cases - Hence, present appeal - Whether Appellant entitled for anticipatory bail.

Facts:

CBI registered FIR under Section 120B Indian Penal Code read with Section 420 Indian Penal Code, Section 8 and Section 13(2) read with Section 13(1)(d) of the Prevention of Corruption Act, 1988 against the Accused for the alleged irregularities in giving FIPB's clearance to company to receive overseas funds. On the basis of the said FIR registered by CBI, the Enforcement Directorate registered a case against the Accused persons for allegedly committing the offence punishable under Sections 3 and 4 of Act. The Appellant moved High Court seeking anticipatory bail in both cases. The High Court dismissed the application refusing to grant anticipatory bail to the Appellant by holding that it was a classic case of money-laundering. The Single Judge dismissed the application for anticipatory bail by holding that the alleged irregularities committed by the Appellant makes out a prima facie case for refusing pre-arrest bail to the Appellant.

Held, while dismissing the appeal:

(i) In terms of Section 4 of the PMLA, the offence of money-laundering was punishable with rigorous imprisonment for a term not less than three years extending to seven years and with fine. The Second Schedule to the Code of Criminal Procedure relates to classification of offences against other laws and in terms of the Second Schedule of the Code, an offence which is punishable with imprisonment for three years and upward but not more than seven years is a cognizable and non-bailable offence. Thus, Section 4 of the Act read with the Second Schedule of the Code makes it clear that the offences under the PMLA are cognizable offences. Section 420 of Indian Penal Code, Section 8 of the Prevention of Corruption Act was then found a mention in Part A of the Schedule. Section 420 Indian Penal Code, Section 8 of the Prevention of Corruption Act is punishable for a term extending to seven years. Thus, the essential requirement of Section 45 of PMLA Accused of an offence punishable for a term of imprisonment of more than three years under Part A of the Schedule was satisfied making the offence under PMLA. There was no merit in the contention of the Appellant that very registration of the FIR against the Appellant under PMLA was not maintainable. [43]

(ii) As rightly submitted by Respondent that if the Accused were to be confronted with the materials which were collected by the prosecution/ Enforcement Directorate with huge efforts, it would lead to devastating consequences and would defeat the very purpose of the investigation into crimes, in particular, white collar offences. If the contention of the Appellant was to be accepted, the investigating agency would have to question each and every Accused such materials collected during investigation and in this process, the investigating agency would be exposing the evidence collected by them with huge efforts using their men and resources and this would give a chance to the Accused to tamper with the evidence and to destroy the money trail apart from paving the way for the Accused to influence the witnesses. If the contention of the Appellant was to be accepted that the Accused would have to be questioned with the materials and the investigating agency has to satisfy the court that the Accused was evasive during interrogation, the court would have to undertake a mini trial of scrutinizing the matter at intermediary stages of investigation like interrogation of the Accused and the answers elicited from the Accused and to find out whether the answers given by the Accused are evasive or whether they were satisfactory or not. This could have never been the intention of the legislature either under PMLA or any other statute. [58]

(iii) Grant of anticipatory bail at the stage of investigation may frustrate the investigating agency in interrogating the Accused and in collecting the useful information and also the materials which might have been concealed. Success in such interrogation would elude if the Accused knows that he is protected by the order of the court. Grant of anticipatory bail, particularly in economic offences would definitely hamper the effective investigation. Having regard to the materials said to have been collected by the Respondent-Enforcement Directorate and considering the stage of the investigation, this court was of the view that it was not a fit case to grant anticipatory bail. [81]

(iv) In a case of money-laundering where it involves many stages of placement, layering i.e. funds moved to other institutions to conceal origin and interrogation i.e. funds used to acquire various assets, it requires systematic and analysed investigation which would be of great advantage. As held in case of Anil Sharma, success in such interrogation would elude if the Accused knows that he is protected by a pre-arrest bail order. Section 438 Code of Criminal Procedure is to be invoked only in exceptional cases where the case alleged is frivolous or groundless. In the case in hand, there were allegations of laundering the proceeds of the crime. The Enforcement Directorate claims to have certain specific inputs from various sources, including overseas banks. Letter rogatory was also said to have been issued and some response have been received by the department. Having regard to the nature of allegations and the stage of the investigation, the investigating agency had to be given sufficient freedom in the process of investigation.

Though this court did not endorse the approach of the Single Judge in extracting the note produced by the Enforcement Directorate, there was no ground warranting interference with the impugned order. Considering the facts and circumstances of the case, grant of anticipatory bail to the Appellant would hamper the investigation and this was not a fit case for exercise of discretion to grant anticipatory bail to the Appellant. [82]

Ratio Decidendi: Grant of anticipatory bail, particularly in economic offences would definitely hamper the effective investigation.

Disposition: In Favour of State.

XI

Nikesh Tarachand Shah vs. Union of India (UOI) and Ors. (23.11.2017 - SC) : MANU/SC/1480/2017

Relative Section:

Prevention of Money-Laundering Act, 2002 - Section 2, Section 3, Section 4,Section 5,Section 5(1),Section 8(2),Section 19, Section 24,Section 43, Section 43(1), Section 44, Section 44(1),Section 45,Section 45(1), Section 46, Section 55, Section 65, Section 71, Section 145;

Prevention of Money-Laundering (Amendment) Act, 2012 [Repealed];

Income Tax Act, 1961 - Section 288; Narcotic Drugs and Psychotropic Substances Act, 1985 - Section 19, Section 24,Section 27A,Section 29,Section 37;

Arms Act 1959; Wild Life (Protection) Act, 1972;

Prevention of Corruption Act, 1988 - Section 5(2),Section 13;

Immoral Traffic (Prevention) Act, 1956;

Terrorist and Disruptive Activities (Prevention) Act, 1987 [Repealed] - Section 20(8);

Indian Evidence Act, 1872 - Section 106; Habeas Corpus Act, 1679; Explosive Substances Act, 1908; Unlawful Activities Prevention Act, 1967 (Central); Explosives Act, 1884; Antiquities and Art Treasures Act 1972; Securities and Exchange Board of India Act, 1992; Customs Act, 1962 - Section

104(1), Customs Act, 1962 - Section 132; Bonded Labour System Abolition Act, 1976; Child and Adolescent Labour (Prohibition and Regulation) Act, 1986; Transplantation of Human Organs and Tissues Act, 1994; Juvenile Justice (Care and Protection of Children) Act, 2000 [Repealed]; Emigration Act, 1983; Passports Act, 1967; Foreigners Act, 1946; Copyright Act, 1957; Trade Marks Act, 1999; Information Technology Act, 2000; Biological Diversity Act, 2002; Protection of Plant Varieties and Farmers-Rights Act, 2001; Environment Protection Act, 1986; Water (Prevention and Control of Pollution) Act, 1974; Air (Prevention and Control of Pollution) Act, 1981; Suppression of Unlawful Acts Against Safety of Maritime Navigation and Fixed Platforms on Continental Shelf Act, 2002; Finance Act, 2015; Finance Act, 2016; Bail Reform Act, 1984; Foreign Exchange Regulation Act, 1973 [Repealed] - Section 35(1); Maharashtra Control of Organised Crime Act, 1999 - Section 21(4);

Code of Criminal Procedure, 1973 (CrPC) - Section 2,Section 173,Section 437,Section 437(1),Section 439, Section 439(1),Section 489A, Section 489B, Section 497, Section 498; Section 120B, Section 121,Section 121A, Section 161, Section 165, Section 165A,Section 232,Section 238,Section 240,Section 251,Section 255, Section 372,Section 373,Section 279,Section 386,Section 388,Section 409,Section 420,Section 471, Indian Section 477A;

Constitution of India - Article 14, Constitution of India - Article 20, Article 21,Article 359(1)

Hon'ble Judges/Coram: Rohinton Fali Nariman and Sanjay Kishan Kaul, JJ.

Equivalent Citation: 2018(181)AIC200, AIR2017SC5500, 2018 (1) ALD(Crl.) 212 (SC), 2018 (102) ACC 960, 2018(1)BomCR(Cri)508, IV(2017)CCR302(SC), 2018CriLJ721, 2017(4)Crimes473(SC), 244 (2017) DLT586, 2018(3)ECrN 325, 2018(360)ELT203(S.C.), 2017/INSC/1137, 2017(4)J.L.J.R.435, 2018(1)JCC114, 2018(1)JLJ45, 2018(2)N.C.C.57, 2018(1)PLJR46, 2018(2)RCR(Criminal)232, 2017(13)SCALE609, (2018) 11 SCC1, 2018 (2) SCJ 353, [2018]145SCL96(SC), [2017]12SCR358

Number of Pages in the Original Judgment: 32
Case Reference:
State of U.P. through C.B.I. v. Amarmani Tripathi MANU/SC/0677/2005 : (2005) 8 SCC 21; Gautam Kundu v. Directorate of Enforcement (Prevention of Money-Laundering Act) MANU/SC/1453/2015 : (2015) 16 SCC 1; Rohit Tandon v. The Enforcement Directorate Criminal Appeal Nos. 1878-1879 of 2017; Rajesh Kumar v. State through Government of NCT of Delhi MANU/SC/1130/ 2011 : (2011) 13 SCC 706; Gurbaksh Singh Sibbia v. State of Punjab MANU/

SC/0215/1980 : (1980) 2 SCC 565; Nagendra v. King-Emperor MANU/WB/0119/1923 : AIR 1924 Cal 476 : 25 Cri LJ 732; K.N. Joglekar v. Emperor MANU/UP/0060/1931 : AIR 1931 All 504 : 33 Cri LJ 94; Emperor v. Hutchinson MANU/UP/0014/1931 : AIR 1931 All 356 : 32 Cri LJ 1271; Gudikanti Narasimhulu v. Public Prosecutor MANU/SC/0089/1977 : (1978) 1 SCC 240 : 1978 SCC (Cri) 115; Gurcharan Singh v. State (Delhi Administration) MANU/SC/0420/1978 : (1978) 1 SCC 118 : 1978 SCC (Cri) 41; State of Bombay and Anr. v. F.N. Balsara MANU/SC/0009/1951 : (1951) SCR 682; Budhan Choudhry v. State of Bihar MANU/SC/0047/1954 : (1955) 1 SCR 1045; Asgarali Nazarali Singaporawalla v. The State of Bombay MANU/SC/0100/1957 : 1957 SCR 678; Kedar Nath Bajoria v. State of West Bengal MANU/SC/0082/1953 : (1954) SCR 30; Shayara Bano v. Union of India and Ors. MANU/SC/1031/2017 : (2017) 9 SCC 1; State of A.P. v. McDowell and Co. MANU/SC/0427/1996 : (1996) 3 SCC 709; Indian Express Newspapers (Bombay) (P) Ltd. v. Union of India MANU/SC/0406/1984 : (1985) 1 SCC 641 : 1985 SCC (Tax) 121; Maneka Gandhi v. Union of India MANU/SC/0133/1978 : (1978) 1 SCC 248; Sunil Batra v. Delhi Admn. MANU/SC/0184/1978 : (1978) 4 SCC 494 : 1979 SCC (Cri) 155; A.K. Gopalan Case MANU/SC/0012/1950 : AIR 1950 SC 27 : (1950) 51 Cri LJ 1383; Siddharam Satlingappa Mhetre v. State of Maharashtra MANU/SC/1021/2010 : (2011) 1 SCC 694; United States v. Anthony Salerno & Vincent Cafaro MANU/USSC/0043/1987 : 481 US 739 (1987); Stack v. Boyle 342 US 1; United States v. Rabinowitz 339 U.S. 56 : S. Ct. 430 : 94 L. Ed. 653 (1950); Kartar Singh v. State of Punjab MANU/SC/1597/1994 : (1994) 3 SCC 569; Ranjitsing Brahmajeetsing Sharma v. State of Maharashtra and Anr. MANU/SC/0268/2005 : (2005) 5 SCC 294; Gorav Kathuria v. Union of India and Ors. MANU/PH/0874/2016 : 2017 (348) ELT 24 (P & H)

Case Note:

Criminal - Grant of bail - Challenged therein - Section 45 of Prevention of Money Laundering Act, 2002 (Act) - Articles 14 and 21 of Constitution of India - Present appeal filed questioning constitutional validity of Section 45 of Act - Whether Section 45 of Act, arbitrary, discriminatory and violative of Appellant's fundamental rights

Facts:

Present appeal was filed questioning constitutional validity of Section 45 of the Act, imposing two conditions for grant of bail. The conditions were that, public prosecutor must be given an opportunity to oppose any application for release on bail and Court must be satisfied, that the Accused was not guilty of such offence, and that he did not commit any offence while on bail.

Held, while disposing of appeal:

(i) Grant of bail would depend upon a circumstance which had nothing to do with the offence of money laundering. On this ground alone, Section 45 would have to be struck down as being manifestly arbitrary and providing a procedure which is not fair or just and would, thus, violate both Articles 14 and 21 of Constitution. [27]

(ii) Another interesting feature of Section 45 was that, twin conditions that need to be satisfied under said Section were that there were reasonable grounds for believing that, accused was not guilty of "such offence" and that he was not likely to commit any offence while on bail. Expression "such offence" would be relatable only to an offence in Part A of Schedule. Thus, in an application made for bail, where offence of money laundering was involved, if Section 45 was to be applied, Court must be satisfied that, there were reasonable grounds for believing that, he was not guilty of the offence under Part A of Schedule, which was not offence of money laundering, but which was a completely different offence. Twin conditions laid down in Section 45 would have no nexus whatsoever with a bail application which concerned itself with offence of money laundering, for if Section 45 was to apply, Court did not apply its mind to whether person prosecuted was guilty of offence of money laundering, but instead applied its mind to whether such person is guilty of scheduled or predicate offence. Bail would be denied on grounds germane to scheduled or predicate offence, whereas person prosecuted would ultimately be punished for a completely different offence- namely, money laundering. This, again, was laying down of a condition which had no nexus with the offence of money laundering at all, and a person who might prove that there were reasonable grounds for believing that, he was not guilty of offence of money laundering might yet be denied bail, because he was unable to prove that, there were reasonable grounds for believing that he was not guilty of scheduled or predicate offence. This would again lead to a manifestly arbitrary, discriminatory and unjust result which would invalidate Section. [28]

(iii) It could not be said that, Section 45 of the Act, imposed two conditions which were akin to conditions that were specified for grant of ordinary bail. It was obvious that, twin conditions set down in Section 45 of Act, were a much higher threshold bar. In fact, presumption of innocence, which was attached to any person being prosecuted of an offence, was inverted by conditions specified in Section 45 of Act, whereas for grant of ordinary bail, presumption of innocence attached. Under Section 45 of Act, Court must be satisfied that, there were reasonable grounds to believe that, person was not guilty of such offence and that he was not likely to commit any offence while on bail. [36]

(iv) Section 45 of Act, was a drastic provision which turns on its head presumption of innocence which was fundamental to a person accused of any offence. Before application of a Section which made drastic inroads into fundamental right of personal liberty guaranteed by Article 21 of Constitution of India, it must be sure that, such provision furthered a compelling State interest for tackling serious crime. Absent any such compelling State interest, indiscriminate application of provisions of Section 45 of Act would certainly violate Article 21 of Constitution. Provisions akin to Section 45 of Act had only been upheld on ground that, there was a compelling State interest in tackling crimes of an extremely heinous nature. [45]

Disposition: Disposed of.

XII

Rohit Tandon vs. The Enforcement Directorate (10.11.2017 - SC) : MANU/ SC/1403/2017

Relative Section:

Prevention of Money-Laundering Act, 2002-Section 2(1),Section 3,Section 4,Section 19,Section 24,Section 44, Section 45,Section 45A,Section 45(1),Section 50,Section 50(4),Section 65,Section 71;

Prevention of Corruption Act, 1988 - Section 12;

Prevention of Money-Laundering (Amendment) Act, 2012 [Repealed];Prevention of Money-Laundering (Amendment) Act, 2005;

Code of Criminal Procedure, 1973 (CrPC) -Section 5,Section 155,Section 172,Section 177(1),Section 439;

Maharashtra Control of Organised Crime Act, 1999 - Section 21(4);

Indian Penal Code, 1860 (IPC) - Section 34, Section 109,Section 120B,Section 188,Section 406, Section 409, Section 420,Section 467,Section 468,Section 471;

Constitution of India - Article 14, Constitution of India - Article 21, Constitution of India - Article 32

Hon'ble Judges/Coram: Dipak Misra, C.J.I., A.M. Khanwilkar and D.Y. Chandrachud, JJ.

Equivalent Citation: 2018(181)AIC141, AIR2017SC5309, 2018 (1) ALD(Crl.) 685 (SC), 2018 (1) ALT (Crl.) 70 (A.P.), 2018(1)BomCR(Cri)487, IV(2017)CCR271(SC), 2018CriLJ416, 2017(4)Crimes220(SC), 2017 (356)ELT3(S.C.), 2017/INSC/1096, 2018-1-LW(Crl)413, 2018(1)N.C.C.634, 2017(13)SCALE385, (2018) 11 SCC46, 2018 (1) SCJ 103, [2018]145SCL1(SC), [2017]13SCR156

Number of Pages in the Original Judgment: 20

Case Reference:

Rakesh Manekchand Kothari v. Union of India Special Criminal Application (Habeas Corpus) No. 4247/2015; Gautam Kundu v. Directorate of Enforcement (Prevention of Money Laundering Act), Government of India MANU/SC/1453/2015 : (2015) 16 SCC 1; Subrata Chattoraj v. Union of India, MANU/SC/0453/2014 : (2014) 8 SCC 768; Y.S. Jagan Mohan Reddy v. CBI MANU/SC/0487/2013 : (2013) 7 SCC 439; Union of India v. Hassan Ali Khan (2011) 10 SCC 235; Ranjitsing Brahmajeetsing Sharma v. State of Maharashtra and Anr. MANU/SC/0268/2005 : (2005) 5 SCC 294; State of Maharashtra v. Vishwanath Maranna Shetty MANU/SC/0982/2012 : (2012) 10 SCC 561; Manoranjana Sinh v. Central Bureau of Investigation MANU/SC/0128/2017 : (2017) 5 SCC 218; Sanjay Chandra v. Central Bureau of Investigation MANU/ SC/1375/2011 : (2012) 1 SCC 40; Gorav Kathuria v. Union of India MANU/ PH/0874/2016; Jignesh Kishorebhai Bajiawala v. State of Gujarat and Ors. MANU/GJ/1035/2017; S.C. Jayachandra v. Enforcement Directorate, Bangalore MANU/KA/0456/2017 : 2017 (349) ELT 392 KAR; Kishin S. Loungani v. UOI and Ors. MANU/KE/2278/2016 : (2017) 1 KHC 355; Pradeep Nirankarnath Sharma v. Directorate of Enforcement MANU/GJ/1110/2017 : 2017 (350) ELT 449 (GUJ); Chhagan Chandrakant Bhujbal v. Union of India and Ors. MANU/MH/2668/2016

Case Note:

Criminal - Rejection of bail - Challenged thereto - Sections 3, 4 and 45 of Prevention of Money Laundering Act, 2002 - Appellant was arrested in connection with criminal case registered under Sections 3 and 4 of Act - Appellant first approached Additional Sessions Judge for releasing him on bail by way of application - Bail application came to be rejected - Appellant thereafter approached High Court by way of bail application and interlocutory application filed therein - High Court rejected prayer for bail vide impugned judgment - Hence, present appeal - Whether Appellant was entitled for enlargement on bail

Facts:

The Appellant was arrested in connection with criminal case registered under Sections 3 and 4 of the Prevention of Money-Laundering Act, 2002. The Appellant first approached the Additional Sessions Judge for releasing him on bail by way of an application. The said bail application came to be rejected vide judgment by the said Court. The Appellant thereafter approached the High Court by way of bail application and an interlocutory application filed therein. The High Court independently considered the merits of the arguments but eventually rejected the prayer for bail vide impugned judgment. Hence, present appeal.

Held, while dismissing the appeal:

(i) The Appellant has not succeeded in persuading us about the inapplicability of the threshold stipulation under Section 45 of the Act. Present Court also noted the inexplicable silence or reluctance of the Appellant in disclosing the source from where such huge value of demonetized currency and also new currency has been acquired by him. The prosecution was relying on statements of many witnesses/accused already recorded, out of which few were considered by High Court. The same makes out a formidable case about the involvement of the Appellant in commission of a serious offence of money-laundering. It was, therefore, not possible for to record satisfaction that there were reasonable grounds for believing that the Appellant was not guilty of such offence. Further, the Lower Courts have justly adverted to the antecedents of the Appellant for considering the prayer for bail and concluded that it was not possible to hold that the Appellant was not likely to commit any offence ascribable to the Act of 2002 while on bail. Since the threshold stipulation predicated in Section 45 has not been overcome, the question of considering the efficacy of other points urged by the Appellant to persuade the Court to favour the Appellant with the relief of regular bail would be of no avail. [27]

(ii) The fact that no limit for deposit was specified, would not extricate the Appellant from explaining the source from where such huge amount has been acquired, possessed or used by him. The volume of demonetized currency recovered from the office and residential premises of the Appellant, including the bank drafts in favour of fictitious persons and also the new currency notes for huge amount, leave no manner of doubt that it was the outcome of some process or activity connected with the proceeds of crime projecting the property as untainted property. No explanation has been offered by the Appellant to dispel the legal presumption of the property being proceeds of crime. Similarly, the fact that the Appellant has made declaration in the Income Tax Returns and paid tax as per law does not extricate the Appellant from disclosing the source of its receipt. No provision in the taxation laws has been brought to notice which grants immunity to the Appellant from prosecution for an offence of money-laundering. In other words, the property derived or obtained by the Appellant was the result of criminal activity relating to a scheduled offence. The argument of the Appellant that there was no allegation in the charge-sheet filed in the scheduled offence case or in the prosecution complaint that the unaccounted cash deposited by the Appellant was the result of criminal activity, would not come to the aid of the Appellant. That would have to be negatived in light of the materials already on record. The possession of such huge quantum of demonetized currency and new currency, without disclosing the source from where it was received and the purpose for which it was received, the Appellant had failed to dispel the legal presumption that he was involved in money-laundering and the property was proceeds of crime. [28]

Disposition: In Favour of State.

XIII

Gautam Kundu vs. Manoj Kumar, Govt. of India (16.12.2015 - SC) : MANU/SC/1453/2015

Relative Section:

Companies Act, 1956 - Section 56, Companies Act, 1956 - Section 67(3), Companies Act, 1956 - Section 117A; Securities and Exchange Board of India Act, 1992 - Section 4, Securities and Exchange Board of India Act, 1992 - Section 11C, Securities and Exchange Board of India Act, 1992 - Section 11C(3), Securities and Exchange Board of India Act, 1992 - Section 12A, Securities and Exchange Board of India Act, 1992 - Section 24, Securities and Exchange Board of India Act, 1992 - Section 26; Prevention of Money-Laundering Act, 2002 - Section 2, Prevention of Money-Laundering Act, 2002 - Section 3, Prevention of Money-Laundering Act, 2002 - Section 4, Prevention of Money-Laundering Act, 2002 - Section 8, Prevention of Money-Laundering Act, 2002 - Section 8(1), Prevention of Money-Laundering Act, 2002 - Section 24, Prevention of Money-Laundering Act, 2002 - Section 44(1), Prevention of Money-Laundering Act, 2002 - Section 45, Prevention of Money-Laundering Act, 2002 - Section 45(1), Prevention of Money-Laundering Act, 2002 - Section 65, Prevention of Money-Laundering Act, 2002 - Section 71; Prevention of Money-Laundering (Amendment) Act, 2012 [Repealed]; Prevention of Money-Laundering (Amendment) Act 2009; Indian Penal Code, 1860 (IPC) - Section

405; Code of Criminal Procedure, 1973 (CrPC) - Section 5, Code of Criminal Procedure, 1973 (CrPC) - Section 439; Securities and Exchange Board of India Rules; Securities and Exchange Board of India Regulations

Hon'ble Judges/Coram: Pinaki Chandra Ghose and R.K. Agrawal, JJ.

Equivalent Citation: 2016(1)ACR550, 2016(158)AIC43, AIR2016SC106, 2016 (92) ACC 931, 2016 ALLMR(Cri)453, 2016(3)BomCR(Cri)35, (2016)2CALLT133(SC), I(2016)CCR39(SC), 121 (2016) CLT645, [2016]195CompCas186(SC), (2016)3CompLJ262(SC), 2016CriLJ666, 2016(4)ECrN 1118, 2016 (334) ELT 195(S.C.), 2016GLH(1)184, 2015/INSC/939, 2016(1)J.L.J.R.291, (2016) 1 MLJ(Crl) 200 (SC), 2016 (1) N.C. C. 466, 2016(1)PLJR445, 2016(1)RCR(Criminal)398, 2016(1)RLW764(SC), 2015(13)SCALE808, (2015) 16 SCC1, 2016 (3) SCJ 123, [2016]133SCL341(SC), [2015]15SCR499

Number of Pages in the Original Judgment: 15

Case Reference:

Afcons Infrastructure Ltd. v. Cherian Verkey Construction Co. (P) Ltd. MANU/SC/0525/2010 : (2010) 8 SCC 24; Gurudevatta VKSSS Maryadit v. State of Maharashtra MANU/SC/0191/2001 : (2001) 4 SCC 534; Visitor, AMU v. K.S. Misra MANU/SC/3792/2007 : (2007) 8 SCC 593; State of Madhya Pradesh v. Baldeo Prasad MANU/SC/0067/1960 : (1961) 1 SCR 970; Harakchand Ratanchand Banthia and Ors. v. Union of India and Ors. MANU/SC/0038/1969 : (1969) 2 SCC 166; A.K. Roy and Ors. v. Union of India and Ors. MANU/SC/0051/1981 : (1982) SCR 272; Subrata Chattoraj v. Union of India and Ors. MANU/SC/0453/2014 : (2014) 8 SCC 768; Y.S. Jagan Mohan Reddy v. Central Bureau of Investigation MANU/SC/0487/2013 : (2013) 7 SCC 439; Union of India v. Hassan Ali Khan MANU/SC/1027/2011 : (2011) 10 SCC 235; Smt. Janata Jha v. Assistant Director, Directorate of Enforcement CRLMC No. 114 of 2011

Case Note:

Criminal - Refusal to grant bail - Appellant - Chairman of Rose Valley - Public Company incorporated and registered under Companies Act, 1956 - Certain non-convertible debentures issued by Rose valley - 'Private placement method' - No advertisements issued to public - Issued to employees, their friends and associates - Fulfilled formalities of private placement - Appellant collected money - Issue of debentures from time to time - Letter issued by SEBI - Informed Appellant about offences alleged to have committed by it - Appeal filed before SAT allowed - Held - Appellant Company had repaid all money collected from investors - Further held - No grounds for violation of Section 11(C)(3) of SEBI Act - Report filed by

Respondent - Alleged commission of offence under Section 24 of SEBI Act - Proceedings challenged in High Court - Pending for hearing - SEBI directed Appellant to refund money to customers of Ashirbad scheme - Order challenged before SAT - Show Cause Notice under Section 8(1) of PMLA served - Appellant filed writ petition before High Court - Challenged notice - Dismissed - Appeal to Division Bench - Dismissed - Division Bench directed Appellant to appear before Adjudicating Authority - Authority to pass a reasoned order - Complaint filed by Respondent in Court of learned Chief Judge, City Sessions Court - Under Section 4 of PMLA - Appellant arrested on suspicion of commission of offence punishable under provisions of PMLA - Detained in custody since - Appellant - Granted bail of father's death - Surrendered later - Filed a fresh bail application - Section 439 of Code of Criminal Procedure - High Court rejected said application - Present Appeal -Whether the provisions of Section 45 of the PMLA are binding on the High Court while considering the application for bail Under Section 439 of the Code of Criminal Procedure - Whether the High Court has exercised its discretion under Section 439 of Code of Criminal Procedure, 1973 capriciously or arbitrarily by refusing bail to the Appellant

Facts:

The Appellant is the Chairman of Rose Valley Real Estate Construction Ltd. (Rose Valley), a public company incorporated in 1999 and registered under the Companies Act, 1956. Certain non-convertible debentures were issued by the Rose Valley by 'private placement method.' No advertisements etc. were issued to the public. The said debentures were issued to the employees of the Company and to their friends and associates after fulfilling the formalities for private placement of debentures. Thus, the Appellant collected money by issuing secured debentures by way of private placement in compliance with the guidelines issued by the Securities and Exchange Board of India (SEBI) from time to time.

In 2013, the Adjudicating Officer, SEBI, passed an order imposing a penalty of Rs. 1 crore upon the Rose Valley for violation of the provisions of Sections 11(C) of the Securities and Exchange Board of India Act, 1992 (the SEBI Act) which was reduced to Rs. 10 lakhs by the Securities Appellate Tribunal. A letter was issued by SEBI to the Appellant informing about the offences alleged to have been committed by it under the Companies Act, SEBI Act & Regulations, and Section 405 of the Indian Penal Code, 1860. The appeal filed by the Appellant before the Securities Appellate Tribunal was allowed holding that the Appellant Company has repaid all the money collected from the investors. It was further held by the Securities Appellate Tribunal that there are no grounds for violation of Section 11(C)(3) of the SEBI Act.

On basis of letter issued by SEBI, the Respondent filed a report, alleging commission of offence by the Rose Valley and its officers, punishable Under Section 24 of the SEBI Act. A complaint was filed by the Respondent authorities, alleging that the Rose Valley transferred the money raised by issue of debentures from the account of one company to that of another company. It is also alleged that the money collected by issuing the debentures for the purpose of one business has been invested in some other business. The proceedings Under Section 24 of the SEBI Act has been challenged in the High Court by way of revision which is pending for hearing and further proceeding of the complaint case, has been stayed by the High Court. The High Court also directed the Respondent not to take any coercive measure against the Appellant.

Vide its order, SEBI directed Appellant Rose Valley to refund the money to the customers of Ashirbad scheme. This order was challenged before the Securities Appellate Tribunal by way of Appeal. A Show Cause Notice Under Section 8(1) of the Prevention of Money Laundering Act, 2002 (PMLA) was served upon Rose Valley and its officials. Rose Valley filed a writ petition before the High Court challenging the said Show Cause Notice. The said writ petition was dismissed by the learned Single Judge of the High Court. Thereafter, the matter was taken in appeal before the Division Bench. The Division Bench dismissed the said appeal and directed the Appellant Rose Valley to appear before the Adjudicating Authority Under Section 8 of the PMLA and directed the Adjudicating Authority to decide the preliminary objections as may be raised by the Rose Valley, including the applicability of the PMLA as also the validity of the search and seizure against Rose Valley. It was further directed that the Adjudicating Authority should pass a reasoned order in the matter and communicate the same to the Appellant.

A complaint was filed by the Respondent in the Court of learned Chief Judge, City Sessions Court against the Appellant Under Section 4 of PMLA, though no offence is made out against the Appellant Under Section 3 of the PMLA. Despite having fully cooperated with the investigation, the Appellant was arrested on suspicion of having committed an offence punishable under the provisions of the PMLA and is detained in custody since then.

While the Appellant was in custody, his father expired upon which he moved an application before the High Court for interim bail to perform the rituals for his deceased father. The High Court directed release of the Appellant on provisional bail for two weeks on the conditions mentioned in the said order. On completion of the period of provisional bail, the Appellant duly surrendered before the Court of learned Chief Judge, City Sessions Court.

In July 2015, Appellant filed a fresh bail application under Section 439 of the Code of Criminal Procedure before the High Court. Vide impugned judgment and order the High Court has rejected the said application of the Appellant holding that no order has yet been passed by any competent Court of law that no offence is made out against the Appellant Under Section 24 of the SEBI Act. A criminal revision praying for quashing of the proceedings initiated against the Appellant Under Section 24 of the SEBI Act is still pending for decision before the High Court. Aggrieved by the rejection of the bail application filed Under Section 439 of the Code of Criminal Procedure, the Appellant has approached this Court through this appeal by special leave.

Held, while dismissing the appeal

1.There is no doubt that PMLA deals with the offence of money laundering and the Parliament has enacted this law as per commitment of the country to the United Nations General Assembly. PMLA is a special statute enacted by the Parliament for dealing with money laundering. Section 5 of the Code of Criminal Procedure, 1973 clearly lays down that the provisions of the Code of Criminal Procedure will not affect any special statute or any local law. In other words, the provisions of any special statute will prevail over the general provisions of the Code of Criminal Procedure in case of any conflict.[28]

2.The conditions specified Under Section 45 of the PMLA are mandatory and needs to be complied with which is further strengthened by the provisions of Section 65 and also Section 71 of the PMLA. Section 65 requires that the provisions of Code of Criminal Procedure shall apply in so far as they are not inconsistent with the provisions of this Act and Section 71 provides that the provisions of the PMLA shall have overriding effect notwithstanding anything inconsistent therewith contained in any other law for the time being in force. PMLA has an overriding effect and the provisions of Code of Criminal Procedure would apply only if they are not inconsistent with the provisions of this Act. Therefore, the conditions enumerated in Section 45 of PMLA will have to be complied with even in respect of an application for bail made Under Section 439 of Code of

Criminal Procedure That coupled with the provisions of Section 24 provides that unless the contrary is proved, the Authority or the Court shall presume that proceeds of crime are involved in money laundering and the burden to prove that the proceeds of crime are not involved, lies on the Appellant.[30]

3.The Court refrained itself from deciding the questions tried to be raised since it is nothing but a bail application. The Court did not forget that this case is relating to "Money Laundering" which it feels is a serious threat to the national economy and national interest. The Court could not brush aside the fact that the schemes have been prepared in a calculative manner with a deliberative design and motive of personal gain, regardless of the consequence to the members of the society.[32]

4.With regard to the questions raised by learned senior Counsel appearing on behalf of the Appellant, at this stage, the Court did not think that it should answer or deal with the same in view of the fact that the matter is pending before a Division Bench of the High Court in writ jurisdiction. Hence, any observation or remarks made by the Court may cause prejudice to the case of both the sides. Therefore, the Court felt that it would be proper for it only to deal with the matter concerning bail.[33]

5.The Court noted that admittedly the complaint is filed against the Appellant on the allegations of committing the offence punishable Under Section 4 of the PMLA. The contention raised on behalf of the Appellant that no offence Under Section 24 of the SEBI Act is made out against the Appellant, which is a scheduled offence under the PMLA, needs to be considered from the materials collected during the investigation by the Respondents. There is no order as yet passed by a competent court of law, holding that no offence is made out against the Appellant Under Section 24 of the SEBI Act and it would be noteworthy that a criminal revision praying for quashing the proceedings initiated against the Appellant Under Section 24 of SEBI Act is still pending for hearing before the High Court.[33]

6.The Court further noted that Section 45 of the PMLA will have overriding effect on the general provisions of the Code of Criminal Procedure in case of conflict between them. Section 45 of the PMLA imposes two conditions for grant of bail, specified under the said Act. The Court has not missed the proviso to Section 45 of the said Act which indicates that the legislature has carved out an exception for grant of bail by a Special Court when any person is under the age of 16 years or is a woman or is a sick or infirm. Therefore, there is no doubt that the conditions laid down Under Section 45A of the PMLA, would bind the High Court as the provisions of special law having overriding effect on the provisions of Section 439 of the Code of Criminal Procedure for grant of bail to any person accused of committing offence punishable Under Section 4 of the PMLA, even when the application for bail is considered Under Section 439 of the Code of Criminal Procedure.[33]

7.The Court could not brush aside the fact that the Appellant floated as many as 27 companies to allure the investors to invest in their different companies on a promise of high returns and funds were collected from the public at large which were subsequently laundered in associated companies of Rose Valley Group and were used for purchasing moveable and immoveable properties.[35]

8.The Court did not intend to further state the other facts excepting the fact that admittedly the complaint was filed against the Appellant on the allegation of committing offence punishable Under Section 4 of the PMLA. The contention made on behalf of the Appellant that no offence Under Section 24 of the SEBI Act is made out against the Appellant, which is a scheduled offence under the PMLA, needs to be considered from the material collected during the investigation and further to be considered by the competent court of law. The Court did not intend to express itself at this stage with regard to the same as it may cause prejudice the case of the parties in other proceedings. The Court was sure that it is not expected at this stage that the guilt of the accused has to be established beyond reasonable doubt through evidences.[36]

9.The Court further noted that the High Court at the time of refusing the bail application, duly considered this fact and further considered the statement of the Assistant General Manager of RBI, Kolkata, seizure list, statements of directors of Rose Valley, statements of officer bearers of Rose Valley, statements of debenture trustees of Rose Valley, statements of debenture holders of Rose Valley, statements of AGM of Accounts of Rose Valley and statements of Regional Managers of Rose Valley for formation of opinion whether the Appellant is involved in the offence of money laundering.[37]

10.In these circumstances, the Court did not find that the High Court exercised its discretion capriciously or arbitrarily in the facts and circumstances of this case. It further noted that the High Court had called for all the relevant papers and duly taken note of that and thereafter after satisfying its conscience, refused the bail. Therefore, the Court did not find that the High Court had committed any wrong in refusing bail in the given circumstances. Accordingly, Court did not find any reason to interfere with the impugned order so passed by the High Court and the bail, as prayed before it, challenging the said order was refused. Consequently the appeal is dismissed. [38]

XIV

P. Mohanraj and Ors. vs. Shah Brothers Ispat Pvt. Ltd. (01.03.2021 - SC) : MANU/SC/0132/2021

Relative Section:

Arbitration Act, 1940 - Section 8(2); Arbitration And Conciliation Act, 1996 - Section 34; Bihar Reorganisation Act, 2000 - Section 89, Bihar Reorganisation Act, 2000 - Section 89(3); Bombay Relief Undertakings (special Provisions) Act, 1958 - Section 2(2), Bombay Relief Undertakings (special Provisions) Act, 1958 - Section 3, Bombay Relief Undertakings (special Provisions) Act, 1958 - Section 4(1);

Code of Criminal Procedure (CrPC), 1861; Code of Civil Procedure, 1908 (CPC) - Order 21 Rule 58,

Code of Civil Procedure, 1908 (CPC) - Section 26;

Code of Criminal Procedure, 1898 (CrPC); Code of Criminal Procedure, 1973 (CrPC) - Section 2(d),Section 4(2),Section 6,Section 29(2),Section 62,Section 63,Section 64, Section 82,Section 173, Section 177, Section 178,Section 179,Section 180,Section 181,Section 182,Section 183,Section 184, Section 185,Section 186, Section 187,Section 188,Section 189,Section 258,Section 264,Section 320,Section 320(1),Section 320(2), Section 320(9),Section 345,Section 357,Section 357(1),Section 357(3),Section 421,Section 431, Section 482; Code of Criminal Procedure, 1974 (CrPC);

Companies Act, 1956 - Section 391, Companies Act, 1956 - Section 442,Section 446,Section 446(1), Section 446(2),Section 454(5),Section 454(5A),Section 457,Section 630,Section 630(1);Section 2;Companies (Amendment) Act, 1960;

Constitution of India - Article 12,Article 19,Article 19(1),Article 19(2),Article 32,Article 132,Article 133,Article 133(1),Article 136,Article 226,Article 233,Article 234,Article 235;

Contempt of Courts Act, 1952; Contempt Of Courts Act, 1971 - Section 2(b), Contempt Of Courts Act, 1971 - Section 11, Section 12,Section 12(1),Section 12(4),Section 12(5),Section 14,Section 15,Section 17,Section 23;

Employees' Provident Funds And Miscellaneous Provisions Act, 1952 - Section 2(e); English And Foreign Languages University Act, 2006 - Section 45(2); Indian Partnership Act, 1932 - Section 69(3);

Indian Penal Code, 1860 (IPC) - Section 53,Section 64,Section 214,Section 364A;

Industrial Disputes Act, 1947 - Section 2(j);

Insolvency And Bankruptcy Code, 2016 - Section 3(18), Section 3(33),Section 5(8),Section 7,Section 8,Section 9,Section 14,Section 14(1),Section 14(2),Section 14(3), Section 14(4),Section 17,Section 25(1),Section 25,Section 25(2),Section 29A,Section 31, Section 31(1),Section 32,Section 32A,Section 32A(1),Section 33, Section 33(5),Section 35,Section 35(1),Section 52,Section 80,Section 81,Section 81(3),Section 84,Section 85, Section 86,Section 91(2),Section 94,Section 95,Section 96,Section 96(1),Section 96(3),Section 100,Section 101, Section 101(1),Section 101(3),Section 114;

Limited Liability Partnership Act 2008 - Section 2;

Negotiable Instruments Act, 1881 - Section 138 to Section 141, Section 141(1), Section 142,Section 142(1), - Section 142(2),Section 143,Section 143A,Section 143A(1),Section 144 to Section 148,Section 148(1),Section 149 to Section 153;

Prevention Of Money-laundering Act, 2002 - Section 14(1); Sick Industrial Companies (special Provisions) Act, 1985 - Section 22, Sick Industrial Companies (special Provisions) Act, 1985 - Section 22(1); State Financial Corporations Act, 1951 - Section 29, State Financial Corporations Act, 1951 - Section 31; Insolvency and Bankruptcy Code (Amendment) Act, 2020; Securitisation and Reconstruction of Financial Assets and Enforcement of Security Interest Act, 2002; Prevention of Corruption Act, 1988; Banking, Public Financial Institutions and Negotiable Instruments Laws (Amendment) Act, 1988; Negotiable Instruments (Amendment and

Miscellaneous Provisions) Act, 2002; General Clauses Act, 1897; Evidence Act; Income-Tax Act, 1961; Indian Companies Act

Hon'ble Judges/Coram: Rohinton Fali Nariman, Navin Sinha and K.M. Joseph, JJ.

Equivalent Citation: 2021(221)AIC1, AIR2021SC1308, 2021 (1) ALD(Crl.) 746 (SC), 2021 (147) ALR 222,2021(2)ALT197, 2021 (2) ALT (Crl.) 105 (A.P.), II(2021)BC27(SC), 2021(2)BLJ312, 2021(3) Bom CR135,2021(2)BomCR(Cri)24, 2021 (1) CCC 371 , (2021)3CompLJ1(SC), 2021(1)Crimes395(SC), 277(2021) DLT428, 2021/INSC/133, 2021 (1) MWN (Cr.) D.C.C. 97, 2021(2)RCR(Criminal)711,2021(2)RCR (Criminal)611, (2021)6SCC258, 2021 (9-10) SCJ 265, [2021]167SCL327(SC), [2021]4SCR204

Number of Pages in the Original Judgment: 68
Case Reference:

Aneeta Hada and Ors. v. Godfather Travels and Tours Pvt. Ltd. and Ors. MANU/SC/0335/2012; State of Assam v. Ranga Mahammad and Ors. MANU/SC/0056/1966; Jagdish Chander Gupta v. Kajaria Traders (India) Ltd. MANU/SC/0047/1964; Rajasthan State Electricity Board, Jaipur v. Mohan Lal and Ors. MANU/SC/0360/1967; C.B.I., Patna and Ors. v. Braj Bhushan Prasad and Ors. MANU/SC/0614/2001; Bangalore Water Supply and Sewerage Board v. A. Rajappa and Ors. MANU/SC/0257/1978; Rohit Pulp and Paper Mills Ltd. v. Collector of Central Excise, Baroda MANU/SC/0186/1991; Oswal Agro Mills Ltd. and Ors. v. Collector of Central Excise and Ors. MANU/SC/0344/1993; K. Bhagirathi G. Shenoy and Ors. v. K.P. Ballakuraya and Ors. MANU/SC/ 0236/1999; Lokmat Newspapers Pvt. Ltd. v. Shankarprasad MANU/SC/0405/ 1999; Godfrey Phillips India Ltd. and Ors. v. State of U.P. and Ors. MANU/ SC/0051/2005; Rainbow Steels Ltd., Muzaffarnagar and Ors. v. C.S.T., U.P. and Ors. MANU/SC/0408/1981; The State of Bombay and Ors. v. The Hospital Mazdoor Sabha and Ors. MANU/SC/0200/1960; Vikram Singh and Ors. v. Union of India (UOI) and Ors. MANU/SC/0901/2015; Siddeshwari Cotton Mills (P) Ltd. v. Union of India (UOI) and Ors. MANU/SC/0359/1989; Tribhuban Parkash Nayyar v. The Union of India (UOI) MANU/SC/0029/ 1969; The U.P. State Electricity Board and Ors. v. Hari Shankar Jain and Ors. MANU/SC/0500/1978; Grasim Industries Ltd. v. Collector of Customs, Bombay MANU/SC/0256/2002; Pioneer Urban Land and Infrastructure Limited and Ors. v. Union of India (UOI) and Ors. MANU/SC/1071/2019; Controller of Estate Duty, Gujarat and Ors. v. Kantilal Trikamlal and Ors. MANU/SC/0520/1976; Subramanian Swamy v. Union of India (UOI) and Ors. MANU/SC/0621/2016; R.L. Arora v. State of Uttar Pradesh and Ors. MANU/

SC/0033/1964; Ahmedabad Pvt. Primary Teachers' Association v. Administrative Officer and Ors. MANU/SC/0032/2004; Swiss Ribbons Pvt. Ltd. and Ors. v. Union of India (UOI) and Ors. MANU/SC/0079/2019; Macquarie Bank Limited v. Shilpi Cable Technologies Ltd. MANU/SC/1609/ 2017; Giriraj Garg v. Coal India Ltd. and Ors. MANU/SC/0212/2019; Goaplast Pvt. Ltd. v. Chico Ursula D'Souza and Ors. MANU/SC/0200/2003; Vinay Devanna Nayak v. Ryot Seva Sahakari Bank Ltd. MANU/SC/0061/2008; Electronics Trade and Technology Development Corpn. Ltd., Secunderabad v. Indian Technologists and Engineers (Electronics) Pvt. Ltd. and Ors. MANU/SC/0591/1996; Damodar S. Prabhu v. Sayed Babalal H. MANU/SC/ 0319/2010; K.M. Ibrahim v. K.P. Mohammed and Ors. MANU/SC/1865/2009; JIK Industries Limited and Ors. v. Amarlal V. Jumani and Ors. MANU/SC/ 0075/2012; Kaushalya Devi Massand v. Roopkishore Khore MANU/SC/0385/ 2011; R. Vijayan v. Baby and Ors. MANU/SC/1245/2011; Dashrath Rupsingh Rathod v. State of Maharashtra MANU/SC/0655/2014; Frick India Ltd. v. Union of India (UOI) and Ors. MANU/SC/0787/1989; Forage and Co. (of Lushala) v. Municipal Corpn. of Greater Bombay and Ors. MANU/SC/0709/ 1999; Lafarge Aggregates and Concrete India P. Ltd. v. Sukarsh Azad and Ors. MANU/SC/1183/2013; Rajneesh Aggarwal v. Amit J. Bhalla MANU/SC/1462/ 2001; Meters and Instruments Private Limited and Ors. v. Kanchan Mehta MANU/SC/1256/2017; Goa Plast (P) Ltd. v. Chico Ursula D'Souza MANU/SC/ 0940/2003; Rangappa v. Mohan MANU/SC/0376/2010; M. Abbas Haji v. T.N. Channakeshava MANU/SC/1302/2019; Zahira Habibulla H. Sheikh and Ors. v. State of Gujarat and Ors. MANU/SC/0322/2004; Abhilash Vinodkumar Jain v. Cox and Kings (India) Ltd. and Ors. MANU/SC/0303/1995; Dulal Chandra Bhar and Ors. v. Sukumar Banerjee and Ors. MANU/WB/0120/1958; Niaz Mohammad and Ors. v. State of Haryana and Ors. MANU/SC/0063/ 1995; T.N. Godavarman Thirumulpad through the Amicus Curiae v. Ashok Khot and Ors. MANU/SC/2520/2006; Sahdeo v. State of U.P. and Ors. MANU/ SC/0132/2010; B.K. Kar v. The Chief Justice and His Companion Judges of The High Court of Orissa and Ors. MANU/SC/0111/1961; Sukhdev Singh Sodhi v. The Hon'ble Chief Justice S. Teja Singh and Ors. MANU/SC/0134/1953; S. Abdul Karim and Ors. v. M.K. Prakash and Ors. MANU/SC/0165/1976; Chhotu Ram v. Urvashi Gulati and Ors. MANU/SC/0492/2001; Anil Ratan Sarkar and Ors. v. Hirak Ghosh and Ors. MANU/SC/0175/2002; Daroga Singh and Ors. v. B.K. Pandey MANU/SC/0336/2004; All India Anna Dravida Munnetra Kazhagam v. L.K. Tripathi and Ors. MANU/SC/0509/2009; Mrityunjoy Das and Ors. v. Sayed Hasibur Rahaman and Ors. MANU/SC/

0177/2001; V.G. Nigam and Ors. v. Kedar Nath Gupta and Ors. MANU/SC/0419/1992; Murray and Co. v. Ashok Kr. Newatia and Ors. MANU/SC/0042/2000; Maninderjit Singh Bitta v. Union of India (UOI) and Ors. MANU/SC/1246/2011; Kanwar Singh Saini v. High Court of Delhi MANU/SC/1111/2011; T.C. Gupta v. Bimal Kumar Dutta and Ors. MANU/SC/1102/2013; BSI Ltd. and Ors. v. Gift Holdings Pvt. Ltd. and Ors. MANU/SC/2443/2000; Maharashtra Tubes Ltd. v. State Industrial and Investment Corporation of Maharashtra Ltd. and Ors. MANU/SC/0427/1993; Kusum Ingots and Alloys Ltd. and Ors. v. Pennar Peterson Securities Ltd. and Ors. MANU/SC/0127/2000; S.V. Kondaskar v. V.M. Deshpande and Ors. MANU/SC/0336/1972; Sudarsan Chits (I) Ltd. v. O. Sukumaran Pillai and Ors. MANU/SC/0037/1984; Central Bank of India v. Elmot Engineering Co. and Ors. MANU/SC/0485/1994; Inderjit C. Parekh and Ors. v. V.K. Bhatt and Ors. MANU/SC/0368/1974; Sheoratan Agarwal and Ors. v. State of Madhya Pradesh MANU/SC/0112/1984; State of Madras v. C.V. Parekh and Ors. MANU/SC/0195/1970; Anil Hada v. Indian Acrylic Limited MANU/SC/0736/1999; U.P. Pollution Control Board v. Modi Distillery and Ors. MANU/SC/0912/1987; State Bank of India v. V. Ramakrishnan MANU/SC/0849/2018 : (2018) 17 SCC 394; Magnhild v. McIntyre Bros. & Co. (1920) 3 KB 321; Allen v. Emerson 1944 IKB 362 : (1944) 1 All ER 344; Hood-Barrs v. IRC (1946) 2 All ER 768 (CA); United Towns Electric Co. Ltd. v. Attorney General for Newfoundland (1939) 1 All ER 423 (PC); Tillmanns and Co. v. S.S. Knutsford Ltd. MANU/MT/0003/1908 : (1908) 2 KB 385 (CA); Attorney General v. Leicester Corporation (1910) 2 Ch 359: (1908-10) All ER Rep Ext 1002; National Assn. of Local Govt. Officers v. Bolton Corpn. 1943 AC 166 : (1942) 2 All ER 425 (HL); Bank of India v. Vijay Transport 1988 Supp SCC 47; Manish Kumar v. Union of India; CIT v. Ishwarlal Bhagwandas (1966) 1 SCR 190; Legal Remembrancer v. Matilal Ghose MANU/WB/0026/1913 : I.L.R. 41 Cal. 173; Andre Paul Terence Ambard v. Attorney-General of Trinidad and Tobago MANU/PR/0109/1936 : AIR 1936 PC 141; D.K. Kapur v. Reserve Bank of India MANU/DE/0038/2001 : (2001) 58 DRJ 424 (DB); Indorama Synthetics (I) Ltd. v. State of Maharashtra MANU/MH/0692/2016 : (2016) 4 Mah LJ 249; Power Grid Corporation of India Ltd. v. Jyoti Structures Ltd. MANU/DE/5162/2017 : (2018) 246 DLT 485; Deputy Director, Directorate of Enforcement Delhi v. Axis Bank MANU/DE/1120/2019 : (2019) 259 DLT 500; Tayal Cotton Pvt. Ltd. v. State of Maharashtra MANU/MH/2352/2018 : (2019) 1 Mah LJ 312; MBL Infrastructure Ltd. v. Manik Chand Somani CRR 3456/2018; Makwana Mangaldas Tulsidas v. State of Gujarat MANU/SC/0517/2020; M. v. Home Office (1993) 3 All ER 537 : (1994) 1 AC 377 : (1993) 3 WLR 433

(HL); H.N. Jagadeesh v. R. Rajeshwari MANU/SCOR/84514/2017

Case Note:

Insolvency -Criminal Proceedings - Moratorium - Scope - Sections 138 and 141 of the Negotiable Instruments Act, 1881 (NI Act) - Section 14 of the Insolvency and Bankruptcy Code, 2016 (IBC) - Cheques issues dishonoured - Criminal complaints initiated followed by proceedings under IBC - Whether proceedings under Section 138 and 141 of the NI Act covered by the moratorium provision under the IBC?

Facts:

The issue involved in the instant case pertains scope of Section 14 of the Insolvency and Bankruptcy Code, 2016 (IBC) vis-Ã-vis proceedings under Sections 138/141 of the Negotiable Instruments Act, 1881 (NI Act). The issue brought up for adjudication was whether criminal proceedings under NI Act would be covered within the scope of moratorium as provided for in IBC. In the present case, several cheques issued in favour of the Respondent were returned dishonoured by reason of insufficient funds. While proceedings were initiated under NI Act, a statutory notice under Section 8 of the IBC was issued by the Respondent to the Company and the Respondent filed a Section 9 petition before the National Company Law Tribunal ('NCLT'). The application was admitted and corporate insolvency resolution process directed to be commenced and moratorium was declared. Thereafter, proceedings in two criminal complaints were stayed. NCLAT set aside the order while holding that Section 138 being a criminal law provision, not a 'proceeding' within the meaning of Section 14 of the IBC. Thereafter, resolution plan was approved as a result of which the moratorium order ceased to have effect. Hence, the present proceedings.

Held, while allowing the Appeals:

A cursory look at Section 14(1) makes it clear that subject to the exceptions contained in Sub-sections (2) and (3), on the insolvency commencement date, the Adjudicating Authority shall mandatorily, by order, declare a moratorium to prohibit what follows in Clauses (a) to (d). Importantly, Under Sub-section (4), this order of moratorium does not continue indefinitely, but has effect only from the date of the order declaring moratorium till the completion of the corporate insolvency resolution process which is time bound, either culminating in the order of the Adjudicating Authority approving a resolution plan or in liquidation. [10]

It can thus be seen that regard being had to the object sought to be achieved by the IBC in imposing this moratorium, a quasi-criminal proceeding which would result in the assets of the corporate debtor being depleted as a result of having to pay compensation which can amount to twice the amount of the cheque that has bounced would directly impact the corporate insolvency resolution process in the same manner as the institution, continuation, or execution of a decree in such suit in a civil court for the amount of debt or other liability. Judged from the point of view of this objective, it is impossible to discern any difference between the impact of a suit and a Section 138 proceeding, insofar as the corporate debtor is concerned, on its getting the necessary breathing space to get back on its feet during the corporate insolvency resolution process. Given this fact, it is difficult to accept that noscitur a sociis or ejusdem generis should be used to cut down the width of the expression "proceedings" so as to make such proceedings analogous to civil suits. [24]

Viewed from another point of view, Clause (b) of Section 14(1) also makes it clear that during the moratorium period, any transfer, encumbrance, alienation, or disposal by the corporate debtor of any of its assets or any legal right or beneficial interest therein being also interdicted, yet a liability in the form of compensation payable Under Section 138 would somehow escape the dragnet of Section 14(1). While Section 14(1)(a) refers to monetary liabilities of the corporate debtor, Section 14(1)(b) refers to the corporate debtor's assets, and together, these two clauses form a scheme which shields the corporate debtor from pecuniary attacks against it in the moratorium period so that the corporate debtor gets breathing space to continue as a going concern in order to ultimately rehabilitate itself. Any crack in this shield is bound to have adverse consequences, given the object of Section 14, and cannot, by any process of interpretation, be allowed to occur. [25]

Since the corporate debtor would be covered by the moratorium provision contained in Section 14 of the IBC, by which continuation of Section 138/141 proceedings against the corporate debtor and initiation of Section 138/141 proceedings against the said debtor during the corporate insolvency resolution process are interdicted. The legal impediment contained in Section 14 of the IBC would make it impossible for such proceeding to continue or be instituted against the corporate debtor. Thus, for the period of moratorium, since no Section 138/141 proceeding can continue or be initiated against the corporate debtor because of a statutory bar, such proceedings can be initiated or continued against the persons mentioned in Section 141(1) and (2) of the Negotiable Instruments Act. This being the case, it is clear that the moratorium provision contained in Section

14 of the IBC would apply only to the corporate debtor, the natural persons mentioned in Section 141 continuing to be statutorily liable under Chapter XVII of the Negotiable Instruments Act[77]

A Section 138/141 proceeding against a corporate debtor is covered by Section 14(1)(a) of the IBC.[78]

Resultantly, the civil appeal is allowed and the judgment under appeal is set aside. [79]

Ratio Decidendi: Proceedings of cheque dishonour under Sections 138/141 of the Negotiable Instruments Act against a corporate debtor covered by Section 14(1)(a) of the Insolvency and Bankruptcy Code.

XV

Union of India (UOI) vs. Hassan Ali Khan and Ors. (30.09.2011 - SC) : MANU/SC/1144/2011

Relative Section:

Code of Criminal Procedure, 1973 (CrPC) - Section 167(2); Code of Criminal Procedure, 1973 (CrPC) - Section 439(2); Indian Evidence Act, 1872 - Section 27, Indian Evidence Act, 1872 - Section 45; Indian Penal Code 1860, (IPC) - Section 121; Indian Penal Code 1860, (IPC) - Section 121A; Prevention Of Money-laundering Act, 2002 - Section 2(u), Prevention Of Money-laundering Act, 2002 - Section 2(y), Prevention Of Money-laundering Act, 2002 - Section 24, Prevention Of Money-laundering Act, 2002 - Section 3, Prevention Of Money-laundering Act, 2002 - Section 3A, Prevention Of Money-laundering Act, 2002 - Section 4, Prevention Of Money-laundering Act, 2002 - Section 45, Prevention Of Money-laundering Act, 2002 - Section 50; Terrorist And Disruptive Activities (prevention) Act, 1987 [repealed] - Section 20(4)(bb)

Hon'ble Judges/Coram: Altamas Kabir and S.S. Nijjar, JJ.

Equivalent Citation: 2012(1)ACR1054(SC), 2012 (77) ACC 278, 2012BomCR(Cri)261, IV(2011) CCR 101 (SC), 2012CriLJ630, 2013(4)Crimes414(SC), 2012(1)ECrN 258, (2012)2GLR1009(SC), (2012) 1MLJ 364(SC), 2012(1)N.C.C.187, 2011(4)RCR(Criminal)427, 2011(11)SCALE302, [2011]109SCL615(SC), [2011] 11 SCR778, 2011(6)UJ4268

Number of Pages in the Original Judgment: 9

Case Reference:

Sanjay Dutt v. State through CBI, Bombay (II) MANU/SC/0554/1994 : (1994) 5 SCC 410; Uday Mohanlal Acharya v. State of Maharashtra MANU/SC/0222/2001 : (2001) 5 SCC 453; State of U.P. v. Amarmani Tripathi MANU/SC/0677/2005 : (2005) 8 SCC 21

Case Note:

Code of Criminal Procedure, 1973 - Section 439--Prevention of Money Laundering Act, 2002--Section 4--Bail--Cancellation-Offence under Section 4--Facts establishing that if respondent No. 1 released on bail--He may abscond--Impugned order of High Court granting bail to said respondent set aside--Bail cancelled.

It is true that at present, there is only a nebulous link between the huge sums of money handled by the respondent No. 1 and any arms deal or intended arms deals, there is no attempt on the part of the respondent No. 1 to disclose the source of the large sums of money handled by him. There is no denying the fact that allegations have been made that the said monies were the proceeds of crime and by depositing the same in his bank accounts, the respondent No. 1 had attempted to project the same as untainted money. The said allegations may not ultimately be established, but having been made, the burden of proof that the said monies were not the proceeds of crime and were not, therefore, tainted shifted to the respondent No. 1 under Section 24 of the Prevention of Money Laundering Act. 2002 (P.M.L. Act).

The High Court having proceeded on the basis that the attempt made by the prosecution to link up the acquisition by the respondent No. 1 of different Passports with the operation of the foreign bank accounts by the said respondent, was not believable, failed to focus on the other parts of the prosecution case. It is true that having a foreign bank account and also having sizeable amounts of money deposited therein does not ipso facto indicate the commission of an offence under the P.M.L. Act, 2002. However, when there are other surrounding circumstances which reveal that there were doubts about the origin of the accounts and the monies deposited therein, the same principles would not apply. The deposit of US$ 700,000 in the Barclays Bank account of the respondent No. 1 has not been denied. On the other hand, the allegation is that the said amount was the proceeds of the sale of diamond Jewellery which is alleged to have been stolen from the collection of the Nizam of Hyderabad. In fact, on behalf of the respondent No. 1. it has been submitted that in respect of the said deal, the respondent

No. 1 had received by way of commission a sum of US$ 30.000 which he had spent in Dubai.

The fact cannot be ignored that the total income of the respondent No. 1 for the assessment years 2001-02 to 2007-08 has been assessed at ` 110,412.68.85.303 by the Income Tax Department and in terms of Section 24 of the P.M.L. Act. the respondent No. 1 had not been able to establish that the same were neither the proceeds of crime nor untainted property. In addition to the above is the other factor involving the notarized document in which the name of Adnan Khashoggi figures.

Lastly, the manner in which the respondent No. 1 had procured three different passports in his name, after his original passport was directed to be deposited, lends support to the apprehension that, if released on bail, the respondent No. 1 may abscond.

Case Category: CRIMINAL MATTERS - CRIMINAL MATTERS RELATING TO BAIL/INTERIM BAIL/ANTICIPATORY BAIL AND AGAINST SUSPENSION OF SENTENCE.

XVI

Suborno Bose vs. Enforcement Directorate and Ors. (05.03.2020 - SC) : MANU/SC/0285/2020

Relative Section:

Excise and Custom Act; Foreign Exchange Management (Realisation, Repatriation and Surrender of Foreign Exchange) Regulations, 2000 - Regulation 6, Foreign Exchange Management (Realisation, Repatriation and Surrender of Foreign Exchange) Regulations, 2000 - Regulation 6(1);

Foreign Exchange Management Act, 1999 - Section 10(5), Section 10(6),Section 13(1),Section 16(3),Section 42,Section 42(1),Section 46,Section 47;

Foreign Exchange Regulation Act, 1973; Orissa Sales Tax Act, 1947 - Section 25; RBI Regulation; Securities and Exchange Board of India Act, 1992

Hon'ble Judges/Coram: A.M. Khanwilkar and Dinesh Maheshwari, JJ.

Equivalent Citation: AIR2020SC4288, [2020]159CLA1(SC), 2020(372)ELT3(S.C.), 2020/INSC/278, (2020)2MLJ646, (2020)14SCC241, [2020]160SCL607(SC), [2020]4SCR60

Number of Pages in the Original Judgment: 12

Case Reference:

The Chairman, SEBI v. Shriram Mutual Fund and Anr. MANU/SC/8185/ 2006; Director of Enforcement v. M/s. MCTM. Corporation Pvt. Ltd. and Ors. MANU/SC/0300/1996; Gujarat Travancore Agency, Cochin v. Commissioner of Income Tax, Kerala, Ernakulam MANU/SC/0332/1989; Securities and Exchange Board of India v. Cabot International Capital Corporation MANU/ MH/0090/2004; Hindustan Steel Ltd. v. State of Orissa MANU/SC/0418/1969

Case Note:

FEMA - Penalty - Determination of liability - Sections 10(6), 42(1), 46 and 47 of Foreign Exchange Management Act, 1999 - Show cause notice was issued to Appellant, stating that Adjudicating Authority was satisfied that there was prima facie contravention of Section 10(6) of FEMA Act read with Sections 46 and 47 of said Act - Reply to show-cause notice filed on behalf of Company including for Appellant - Adjudicating Authority concluded that noticee Company and Appellant had violated Section 10(6) of FEMA Act read with Sections 46 and 47 of Act having found that goods had arrived in India, but Company failed to submit Bill of Entry and did not take delivery of goods - Resultantly, Adjudicating Authority imposed penalty on Appellant and noticee company - Company, as well as, Appellant filed appeals before Appellate authority - Appellate Authority dismissed appeals and was pleased to uphold decision of Adjudicating Authority - Being aggrieved, Company, as well as Appellant carried matter before High Court - Both appeals were dismissed by High Court - Hence, present appeal - Whether Appellant could be made liable for contravention committed by erstwhile management of Company.

Facts:

A show-cause notice was issued to the Appellant, stating that the Adjudicating Authority was satisfied that there was a prima facie contravention of Section 10(6) of the FEMA Act read with Sections 46 and 47 of the said Act and the Foreign Exchange Manual in the complaint filed against the company of which, the Appellant was the Managing Director. The reply to the show-cause notice filed on behalf of the Company including for the Appellant and the submissions made before the Adjudicating Authority were duly considered by the Adjudicating Authority. The Adjudicating Authority concluded that the noticee Company and the Appellant had violated the provisions of Section 10(6) of the FEMA Act read with Sections 46 and 47 of the said Act read with the Foreign Exchange Manual having found that the goods had arrived in India, but the Company failed to submit Bill of Entry and did not take delivery of the goods. The import formalities would have had completed only after submission of Bill of Entry. Thus, though the goods for which foreign exchange was remitted had reached the destination of the users, but the same were not released and as such kept in bonded warehouse. That resulted in contravention warranting issuance of show-cause notice to the Company and the Appellant. Resultantly, the Adjudicating Authority imposed penalty on Appellant and the company. The Company, as well as, the Appellant carried the matter in appeal before the Special Director (Appeals), FEMA and Commissioner of Income-Tax. The Appellate Authority dismissed both the appeals and was pleased to uphold the decision of the Adjudicating Authority. Being aggrieved, the Company, as well as the Appellant carried the matter before the High Court. Both appeals were dismissed by the High Court.

Held, while dismissing the appeals:

(i) The contravention referred to in Section 10(6) of the FEMA Act is a continuing actionable offence. If so, the Company and the persons managing the affairs of the Company remain liable to take corrective measures in right earnest. Considering the admitted fact that the Appellant took over the management of the Company and was fully alive to the default committed by the Company, yet failed to take corrective steps in right earnest. Notably, being conscious of such contravention, the Appellant had sought indulgence of the authorities for more time. It must follow that the Appellant cannot now be heard to contend that no liability could be fastened on him individually. Indeed, Regulation 6 of the FEMA Regulations provides for the period within which the foreign exchange ought to be surrendered if the Company was not wanting to take delivery of the goods imported. That, however, does not mean that the contravention ceased to exist beyond the specified period. On the other hand, after the specified period had expired, it would be a case of deemed contravention until rectified. [11]

(ii) It was not the case of the Appellant that he was not an officer or a person in charge of and responsible to the Company for the conduct of the business of the Company, as well as, the Company on or after he took charge of company. Considering the fact that the Appellant admittedly became aware of the contravention yet failed to take corrective measures until the action to impose penalty for such contravention was initiated, he could not be permitted to invoke the only defence available in terms of proviso to Sub-Section (1) of Section 42 of the FEMA Act that the contravention took place without his knowledge or that he exercised all due diligence to prevent such contravention. In the reply filed to the show-cause notice by the Appellant, no such specific plea had been taken. [12]

(iii) Therefore, no error had been committed by the Adjudicating Authority in finding that the Appellant was also liable to be proceeded with for the contravention by the Company of which he became the Managing Director and for penalty therefor as prescribed for the contravention of Section 10(6) read with Sections 46 and 47 of the FEMA Act read with the Foreign Exchange Manual. The First Appellate Authority and the High Court justly affirmed the view so taken by the Adjudicating Authority. [15]

Disposition: Appeal Dismissed.

XVII

Union of India (UOI) and Ors. vs. Premier Limited and Ors. (29.01.2019 - SC) : MANU/SC/0094/2019

Relative Section:

Foreign Exchange Regulation Act, 1973 [Repealed] - Section 50; Foreign Exchange Regulation Act, 1973 [Repealed] - Section 51, Foreign Exchange Regulation Act, 1973 [Repealed] - Section 52, Foreign Exchange Regulation Act, 1973 [Repealed] - Section 54, Foreign Exchange Regulation Act, 1973 [Repealed] - Section 81; Foreign Exchange Management Act, 1999 - Section 17 to Section 19,Section 49

Hon'ble Judges/Coram: Abhay Manohar Sapre and Indira Banerjee, JJ.

Equivalent Citation: 2019(2)ALLMR939, 2019(2)BomCR860, [2019]150CLA1(SC), [2019] 213 CompCas1(SC), 2020(1)CWC751, 2019 (365)ELT657(S.C.), 2019/INSC/102, 2019(3)KarLJ418, (2019) 2MLJ483, 2019(2)SCALE373, (2020)14SCC492, 2019 (5) SCJ 118, [2019]152SCL226(SC), [2019]2SCR55

Number of Pages in the Original Judgment: 15

Case Reference:

Foreign Exchange Regulation Act, 1973 [Repealed] - Section 9(1), Foreign Exchange Regulation Act, 1973 [Repealed] - Section 13, Foreign Exchange Regulation Act, 1973 [Repealed] - Section 16(1), Foreign Exchange Regulation

Act, 1973 [Repealed] - Section 17, Foreign Exchange Regulation Act, 1973 [Repealed] - Section 18(1), Foreign Exchange Regulation Act, 1973 [Repealed] - Section 18A, Foreign Exchange Regulation Act, 1973 [Repealed] - Section 19(1), Foreign Exchange Regulation Act, 1973 [Repealed] - Section 50, Foreign Exchange Regulation Act, 1973 [Repealed] - Section 51, Foreign Exchange Regulation Act, 1973 [Repealed] - Section 52, Foreign Exchange Regulation Act, 1973 [Repealed] - Section 52(1), Foreign Exchange Regulation Act, 1973 [Repealed] - Section 52(2), Foreign Exchange Regulation Act, 1973 [Repealed] - Section 52(3), Foreign Exchange Regulation Act, 1973 [Repealed] - Section 52(4), Foreign Exchange Regulation Act, 1973 [Repealed] - Section 52(5), Foreign Exchange Regulation Act, 1973 [Repealed] - Section 52(6), Foreign Exchange Regulation Act, 1973 [Repealed] - Section 54, Foreign Exchange Regulation Act, 1973 [Repealed] - Section 55, Foreign Exchange Regulation Act, 1973 [Repealed] - Section 60, Foreign Exchange Regulation Act, 1973 [Repealed] - Section 81; Foreign Exchange Management Act, 1999 - Section 16, Foreign Exchange Management Act, 1999 - Section 17, Foreign Exchange Management Act, 1999 - Section 17(1), Foreign Exchange Management Act, 1999 - Section 18, Foreign Exchange Management Act, 1999 - Section 19, Foreign Exchange Management Act, 1999 - Section 19(2), Foreign Exchange Management Act, 1999 - Section 28(2), Foreign Exchange Management Act, 1999 - Section 35, Foreign Exchange Management Act, 1999 - Section 49, Foreign Exchange Management Act, 1999 - Section 49(1), Foreign Exchange Management Act, 1999 - Section 49(5), Foreign Exchange Management Act, 1999 - Section 49(5)(2); Foreign Exchange Regulation Act, 1947 - Section 23, Foreign Exchange Regulation Act, 1947 - Section 23E(2), Foreign Exchange Regulation Act, 1947 - Section 23E(3), Foreign Exchange Regulation Act, 1947 - Section 23E(4); General Clauses Act 1897 - Section 6; Smugglers and Foreign Exchange Manipulators (Forfeiture of Property) Act, 1976 - Section 12(1); Finance Act, 2017; Indian Penal Code, 1860 (IPC) - Section 193, Indian Penal Code, 1860 (IPC) - Section 228; Code of Criminal Procedure, 1973 (CrPC) - Section 345, Code of Criminal Procedure, 1973 (CrPC) - Section 346

Case Note:

FERA - Jurisdiction - Present appeal was filed by Union of India against final judgment of High Court holding that, appeals filed by Respondent Nos. 2 to 4 before Special Director (Appeals) against adjudication order were maintainable as Special Director (Appeals) possessed jurisdiction to decide appeals on merits - if Adjudicating Officer had passed an order after repeal of FERA in proceedings initiated prior to 1st June, 2000, whether an appeal against such order would lie before "Special Director (Appeals)" under Section 17 of FEMA or before "Appellate Tribunal" under Section 19 of FEMA.

Facts:

On 1st May, 1991, a memorandum to show cause notice was issued by Special Director to Respondent Nos. 2, 3 and 4, namely, M/s. Godrej Industries Ltd. [formerly known as Godrej Soaps Ltd. (R-2)] and its two Directors (R-3 and R-4) for allegedly committing contravention of Sections 9 (1) (a), 9(1)(c) and Section 16(1) of Foreign Exchange Regulation Act, 1973 (hereinafter referred to as "FERA") in respect of imports and exports of certain commodities made with two foreign parties, viz., M/s. Fingrain, S.A., Geneva and M/s. Continental Grain Export Corporation, New York during the year 1977-78. During pendency of proceedings, FERA was repealed with effect from 1st June, 2000. It was, however, replaced by Foreign Exchange Management Act, 1999 ("FEMA"). On 5th December, 2003, an adjudication order was passed by Deputy Director of Enforcement under FEMA read with FERA in relation to show cause notice dated 1st May, 1991. By this order, penalty of Rs. 15,50,000 was imposed on M/s. Godrej Industries Ltd. and its two Directors for contravening the provisions of Sections 9 (1)(a) and 9(1)(c) read with Section 16 (1) of FERA. On 15th January, 2004, Respondent Nos. 2 to 4 felt aggrieved by adjudication order dated 5th December, 2003 and filed appeal before Special Director (Appeals) under Section 17 of FEMA. Special Director (Appeals) dismissed appeals as being not maintainable holding that, Special Director (Appeals) had no jurisdiction to hear appeals against adjudication order passed under Section 51 of FERA. Respondent Nos. 2 to 4 felt aggrieved by orders and filed writ petitions before High Court. By impugned common order, High Court allowed writ petitions and quashed orders of Special Director (Appeals). High Court held that, appeals filed by Respondent Nos. 2 to 4 before Special Director (Appeals) against adjudication order were maintainable as Special Director (Appeals) possessed jurisdiction to decide appeals on merits. It was against this order of High Court, Revenue had felt aggrieved and filed present appeal by way of special leave before present Court.

Held, while allowing the appeal

1. Any appeal filed after 1st June, 2000 against order of Adjudicating Officer passed under Section 51 of FERA in proceedings initiated under FERA would lie before Appellate Tribunal under Section 19 of FEMA. [22]

2. If Adjudicating Officer had passed order under Section 51 of FERA prior to 1st June, 2000 when FERA was in force, appeal against such order was

maintainable only under Section 52 (2) before Appellate Board under FERA. [23]

3. If such appeal had remained pending before Appellate Board on 1st June, 2000, same would have been transferred to Appellate Tribunal constituted under FEMA in terms of Section 49 (5)(b) of FEMA for its disposal. [24]

4. A fortiori, any appeal, if filed after 1st June, 2000 and against similar order, i.e., an order passed under Section 51 of FERA should also be held to lie before Appellate Tribunal Under Section 19 of FEMA alike appeals filed prior to 1st June, 2000 and which were transferred to Appellate Tribunal by virtue of Section 49(5)(b) of FEMA. [26]

5. Reason behind this simultaneous statutory transfer of pending appeals to Appellate Tribunal under FEMA appeared to be that legislature did not intend to provide two separate Appellate Authorities under FEMA for challenging adjudication order passed under Section 51 of FERA, i.e., one appeal before Special Director (Appeals) and other appeal before Appellate Tribunal under FEMA. [27]

6. Legislature did not intend to make a distinction between two appeals for their disposal by two different appellate authorities under FEMA only because one appeal was filed prior to 1st June, 2000, therefore, it would lie before Appellate Tribunal whereas other appeal which was filed after 1st June, 2000 though against similar order, it would lie before Special Director (Appeals). There did not appear to be any justifiable reason to make such distinction for filing of appeals filed against similar order passed under FERA before two different appellate authorities under FEMA. [28]

7. Perusal of Scheme of FEMA would show that, Special Director (Appeals) was subordinate in hierarchy to Appellate Tribunal prescribed under Section 49(5)(2) of FEMA. It was, therefore, not possible to hold that, one appeal would be maintainable before the Appellate Tribunal and other appeal arising out of similar order would be maintainable before Special Director (Appeals), who was subordinate in hierarchy to Appellate Board. Such distinction did not stand for any logic. [37]

8. Appellate forum for deciding appeals arising out of order passed under Section 51 of FERA whether filed prior to 1st june, 2000 or filed after 1st June, 2000 must be same, i.e., Appellate Tribunal under FEMA. [40]

9. Appeal filed by Respondent Nos. 2 to 4 against order dated 5th December, 2003 passed by Deputy Director of enforcement under Section 51 of FERA would lie and was, therefore, maintainable only before Appellate

Tribunal under Section 19 of FEMA. [41]

10. Appeals which Respondent Nos. 2 to 4 had filed before Special Director (Appeals) were accordingly transferred to concerned Appellate Tribunal constituted under Section 18 of FEMA for their disposal on merits in accordance with law. [42]

11. Appeal allowed. Impugned order was set aside. [43]

Disposition: Appeal Allowed.

XVIII

Union of India (UOI) and Ors. vs. S. Srinivasan (21.05.2012 - SC) : MANU/ SC/0496/2012

Relative Section: Advocate Act, 1961 - Section 2 (a);

Constitution Of India - Article 136,Article 14,Article 16,Article 233,Article 233(2),Article 234,Article 235, Article 236,Article 236(b);

Foreign Exchange Management Act, 1999 - Section 15, Section 16,Section 17,Section 18,Section 19,Section 2(s),Section 20,Section 20(1),Section 21,Section 21(1),Section 21(1)(b),Section 21(2)(a),Section 22,Section 23, Section 25,Section 26,Section 27,Section 28,Section 39,Section 46,Section 46(2), Section 5; Foreign Exchange Regulation Act, 1973 [repealed] - Section 52

Hon'ble Judges/Coram: B.S. Chauhan and Dipak Misra, JJ.

Equivalent Citation: 2012(116)AIC150, 2012(281)ELT3(S.C.), 2012(3)ESC401(SC), 2012-4-LW567, 2012(5)SCALE702, (2012)7SCC683, [2012]114SCL441(SC), [2012]6SCR34, 2012(3)SLJ250(SC

Number of Pages in the Original Judgment: 13

Case Reference:

Chander Mohan v. State of Uttar Pradesh and Ors. MANU/SC/0052/1966 : (1967) 1 SCR 77; State of Maharashtra v. Labour Law Practitioners' Association and Ors. MANU/SC/0121/1998 : (1998) 2 SCC 688; Union of India and Anr. v. Delhi High Court Bar Association and Ors. MANU/SC/0194/2002

: (2002) 4 SCC 275; General Officer Commanding-in-Chief v. Dr. Subhash Chandra Yadav MANU/SC/0165/1988 : AIR 1988 SC 876 : AIR 1966 SC 1987; Additional District Magistrate (Rev.) Delhi Administration v. Ram AIR 2000 SC 2143; Sukhdev Singh v. Bhagat Ram MANU/SC/0667/1975 : AIR 1975 SC 1331; State of Karnataka and Anr. v. H. Ganesh Kamath etc. MANU/SC/0269/ 1983 : AIR 1983 SC 550; Kunj Behari Lal Butail and Ors. v. State of H.P. and Ors. MANU/SC/0111/2000 : AIR 2000 SC 1069; St. Johns Teachers Training Institute v. Regional Director MANU/SC/0092/2003 : AIR 2003 SC 1533; Global Energy Ltd. and Anr. v. Central Electricity Regulatory Commission MANU/SC/0979/2009 : (2009) 15 SCC 570; State of T.N. and Anr. v. P. Krishnamurthy and Ors. MANU/SC/1581/2006 : (2006) 4 SCC 517; Pratap Chandra Mehta v. State Bar Council of Madhya Pradesh and Ors. MANU/SC/ 0912/2011 : (2011) 9 SCC 573; Satya Narian Singh v. High Court of Judicature at Allahabad and Ors. MANU/SC/0069/1984 : (1985) 1 SCC 225; Rameshwar Dayal v. State of Punjab MANU/SC/0313/1960 : AIR 1961 SC 816; Kumar Padma Prasad v. Union of India and Ors. MANU/SC/0227/1992 : (1992) 2 SCC 428; Sushma Suri v. Govt. of National Capital Territory of Delhi and Anr. MANU/SC/0642/1998 : (1999) 1 SCC 330; Oma Shanker Sharma v. Delhi Administration CWP No. 1961 of 1987; Gokaraju Rangaraju v. State of Andhra Pradesh MANU/SC/0143/1981 : AIR 1981 SC 1473; M.M. Gupta and Ors. v. State of J. & K. and Ors. MANU/SC/0033/1982 : AIR 1982 SC 1579

Case Note:

FEMA - Legality of Order - Rules 2 (1) (b) and 5 of Foreign Exchange (Recruitment, Salary and Allowances and Other Conditions of Service of Chairperson and Members) Rules, 2000; Sections 20, 21, 21(1)(b), 21(2)(a) and 46 Foreign Exchange Management Act, 1999; Article 233 of Constitution of India, 1950 - High Court declared first and second proviso to Rule 5 of Rules, as ultra vires Section 21(1)(b) of Act, and quashed appointments of Respondent Nos. 3 and 4 who were appointed as part time Members and further quashed appointment of Respondent No. 3 as acting Chairperson of Appellate Tribunal - Hence, present Appeals - Whether impugned order was illegal - Held, there was no conception of a part time Member under scheme of Act - A person, in order to be qualified for appointment as Chairperson, was required to be or had been qualified to be a Judge of High Court and a person to be a Member was required to be or had been qualified to be a district judge and to be appointed as a Special Director (Appeal), he had to be a member of the Indian Legal Service and was required to have held a post of Grade I or that service or a member of Indian Revenue Service as a post equivalent to Joint Secretary to Government of India - Thus, a member of Indian Legal Service who was qualified as per Section 21(2)(a) of Act, was entitled to be appointed as a Special Director (Appeal) - There were three distinctive forums for adjudication and there was a hierarchical system - Section 46 of Act, provided for rule making power - If a rule went beyond rule making power conferred by statute, then same had to be declared ultra vires - If a rule supplanted any provision for which power had not been conferred, it became ultra vires - Basic test was to determine and consider source of power which was relatable to rule - A rule must be in accord with parent statute as it could not travel beyond it - In case of Additional District Magistrate (Rev.) Delhi Administration v. Shri Ram, it had been ruled that, conferment of rule making power by an Act did not enable rule making authority to make a rule which traveled beyond scope of enabling Act or which was inconsistent therewith or repugnant thereto - Section 20 of Act, dealt with composition of Appellate Tribunal - Section 21 of Act, dealt with qualification for appointment of Chairperson, Member and Special Director (Appeals) - Appellate Tribunal had been conferred jurisdiction to decide an Appeal from Appellate Tribunal and it had to deal with matters relating to foreign exchange - If object and purpose of Act was to confer power on Appellate Board to deal with issue of economy under scheme of Act, it was well nigh impossible to conceive of appointment of a part time Member - Section 20 of Act, enabling provision, empowered Central Government to fix such number of persons as Government might deem fit - Main part of Rule 5 of Rules, provided that a tribunal would have one Chairperson and Members not exceeding four - To that extent, it was in consonance with Act and it came within framework of provision - First proviso stipulated that, number of either full time Members or part time Members would not exceed two - This proviso introduced concept of part time Member - It traveled beyond enabling provision and was totally inconsistent with it - Rule did not conform to main enactment - Therefore, High Court was justified in declaring said provision as ultra vires - Second proviso was an innovative one - It provided for qualification of a part time Member who could be appointed from amongst officers belonging to Indian Legal Service who fulfilled qualification prescribed under Clause (b) of Sub-Rule (1) of Rule 2 of Rules - Clause (b) of Sub-Rule (1) of Rule 2 of Rules, spelled out that a person would not be qualified for appointment as a Member unless, he was or had been or was qualified to be a district judge - Article 233 of Constitution, dealt with appointment of district judges - It provided for qualification to be a district judge - Rule 2 (1) (b) of Rules, provided qualification to be a Member - Same was in total accord with Act - First proviso to Rule 5 of Rules, introduced part time Member - Said proviso, as far as it introduced concept of part time Member, was contrary to provision contained in enabling Act - Section 46 of Act, nowhere envisaged about part time Members - Second proviso was an innovative one - There could not be a part time Member - A person who was qualified to be a district judge could be a Member if he met criterion laid down in pronouncements of this Court - They were strictly followed - There was no justification for introduction of second proviso to bring in officers from Indian Legal Service who were qualified to become district judges to be part time Members - If officer satisfied requisite qualification, he could be appointed as a Member - Therefore, second proviso had been incorporated to bring in only part time Members and once introduction of part time Members was treated to be ultra vires Act, rest part of Rule was redundant - If officer belonging to Indian Legal Services was qualified to be a district judge, he could compete and be selected for post of Member and that qualification was to be in accord with pronouncements of law of this Court - High Court had quashed appointment of part time Members and appointment of Chairperson who was a part time Member once - As appointment of part time Member was quashed, as a logical corollary, such a person could not be allowed to be appointed to post of Chairperson - Disqualified Member could not hold post of a Chairperson as a stop gap arrangement - Thus, there was no error in that regard in judgment passed by High Court - Appeals disposed

Case Category:

STATUTORY APPOINTMENTS - APPOINTMENT OF CHAIRMAN, VICE-CHAIRMAN AND MEMBERS OF STATUTORY CORPORATIONS/BODIES

Facts:

1. Though prayers in different writ petitions were couched differently, yet the three basic reliefs which were sought before the High Court are - Rule 5 of the Appellate Tribunal for Foreign Exchange (Recruitment, Salary and Allowances and Other Conditions of Service of Chairperson and Members) Rules, 2000 (hereinafter referred to as 'the Rules') is ultra vires the Foreign Exchange Management Act, 1999 (for brevity 'the Act'); for quashment of certain notifications issued by the Government of India, Ministry of Law, Justice and Company Affairs, appointing part time Members of the Appellate Tribunal by issue of a writ of quo warranto as they did not satisfy the eligibility criteria as stipulated in the Act; and further to quash the

appointment of Respondent No. 3 to act as the Chairperson as he was a part time Member and also was not eligible to hold the post.[2]

2. It was urged before the High Court that the Rule travels beyond the scope and ambit of the Act and, in fact, directly runs counter to the provisions in the Act and, therefore, deserves to be declared as ultra vires. It was canvassed that when the Act did not conceive of part time Members, even a person meeting the eligibility criteria could not be appointed as a part time Member. It was further propounded before the High Court that a part time Member who was disqualified to hold the post could not have been allowed to act as the Chairperson as that would destroy the spirit of the Act. To bolster the said submissions, the Petitioners before the High Court placed reliance on Chander Mohan v. State of Uttar Pradesh and Ors. MANU/SC/ 0052/1966 : (1967) 1 SCR 77, Shri Kumar Padma Prasad v. Union of India and Ors. MANU/SC/0227/1992 : (1992) 2 SCC 428 and State of Maharashtra v. Labour Law Practitioners' Association and Ors. MANU/SC/0121/1998 : (1998) 2 SCC 688.[2]

3. The contentions raised by the Petitioners before the writ court were resisted by the Respondent on the ground that the Members of Indian Legal Services were only required to hold the post of part time Member and, therefore, the rule does not really run counter to the Act in question; that as a stopgap arrangement, a part time Member could be appointed as the Chairperson of the Appellate Tribunal and hence, no facet could be found fault with such an appointment; and that a writ of quo warranto could not be issued as the persons, who were meeting the eligibility criteria had been appointed by a High Level Committee. Reliance was placed on the decision in Union of India and Anr. v. Delhi High Court Bar Association and Ors. MANU/SC/0194/2002 : (2002) 4 SCC 275.[3]

4. The High Court declared the first and second proviso to Rule 5 of the Rules as ultra vires Section 21(1)(b) of the Act and quashed the appointments of Respondent Nos. 3 and 4 who were appointed as part time Members and further quashed the appointment of Respondent No. 3 as the acting Chairperson of the Appellate Tribunal.[5]

Held, while allowing the appeal

1. At this juncture, we are obliged to clarify the position further. This Court while issuing notice had granted stay on the operation of the judgment. We have been apprised by Mr. Bhatt that the Central Government, at present, has been scrupulously following the mandate of the Act and only qualified persons are appointed as Members and Chairperson. To avoid any

confusion, we clarify that the judgments and orders passed by the Appellate Tribunal by the Chairperson or Members who were not qualified and whose appointments have been quashed shall not be treated to be null and void. In this regard we may refer with profit the decisions in Gokaraju Rangaraju v. State of Andhra Pradesh MANU/SC/0143/1981 : AIR 1981 SC 1473 and M.M. Gupta and Ors. v. State of J. & K. and Ors. MANU/SC/0033/1982 : AIR 1982 SC 1579 wherein this Court, while quashing the appointments of the Respondents, had clarified that the orders and judgments delivered by them during the period they had continued to function as district judges on the basis of invalid appointments could not be rendered as legally invalid and void. In the larger interest of justice, they are treated as valid and binding. Relying on the said dictum, we clarify the position accordingly.[35]

2. The appeals stand disposed of without any order as to costs.[36]

XIX

Thirumalai Chemicals Limited vs. Union of India (UOI) and Ors. (11.04.2011 - SC) : MANU/ SC/0427/2011

Relative Section:

Constitution Of India - Article 226, Constitution Of India - Article 227; Foreign Exchange Management Act, 1999 - Section 13, Foreign Exchange Management Act, 1999 - Section 19, Foreign Exchange Management Act, 1999 - Section 19(1), Foreign Exchange Management Act, 1999 - Section 19(2), Foreign Exchange Management Act, 1999 - Section 49, Foreign Exchange Management Act, 1999 - Section 49(5) (a), Foreign Exchange Management Act, 1999 - Section 49(5)(a); Foreign Exchange Regulation Act, 1973 [repealed] - Section 50, Foreign Exchange Regulation Act, 1973 [repealed] - Section 51, Foreign Exchange Regulation Act, 1973 [repealed] - Section 52, Foreign Exchange Regulation Act, 1973 [repealed] - Section 52(2), Foreign Exchange RegulationAct, 1973 [repealed] - Section 8(3), Foreign Exchange Regulation Act, 1973 [repealed] - Section 8(4); General Clauses Act 1897 - Section 6; Limitation Act, 1963 - Section 5

Hon'ble Judges/Coram: R.V. Raveendran and K.S. Panicker Radhakrishnan, JJ.

Equivalent Citation: 2011(101)AIC53, AIR2011SC1725, 2011 5 AWC4585SC, 2012(1)BomCR790, [2011]102CLA269(SC), [2011]163CompCas380(SC), (2011)3CompLJ46(SC), (2011)3CompLJ46(SC), 2011 (268)ELT296(S.C.), JT2011(4)SC453, 2011(4)KCCRSN395, 2011(3)RCR(Civil)20, 2011(4)SCALE642, (2011)6SCC739, [2011]108SCL78(SC), [2011]4SCR838, 2011(2)UJ1670

Number of Pages in the Original Judgment: 12

Case Reference:

Harbanslal Sahnia and Anr. v. IOC Ltd. and Ors. MANU/SC/1199/2002 : (2003) 2 SCC 107; L.K. Verma v. HMT Ltd. and Anr. MANU/SC/0703/2006 : (2006) 2 SCC 269; Garikapati Veeraya v. N. Subbiah Choudhry and Ors. MANU/SC/0008/1957 : AIR 1957 SC 540; New India Insurance Company Limited v. Smt. Shanti Mishra MANU/SC/0547/1975 : (1975) 2 SCC 840; Hitendra Vishnu Thakur and Ors. v. State of Maharashtra and Ors. MANU/SC/0526/1994 : (1994) 4 SCC 602; Maharaja Chintamani Saran Nath Shahdeo v. State of Bihar and Ors. MANU/SC/0643/1999 : (1999) 8 SCC 16; Shyam Sundar and Ors. v. Ram Kumar and Anr. MANU/SC/0405/2001 : (2001) 8 SCC 24; The King v. Chandra Dharma (1905) 2 KB 335; Yew Bon Tew v. Kenderaan Bas Mara (1982) 3 All E.R. 833; Anant Gopal Sheorey v. State of Bombay MANU/SC/0046/1958 : AIR 1958 SC 915; Rao Shiv Bahadur Singh and Anr. v. State of Vindhya Pradesh MANU/SC/0081/1953 : AIR 1953 SC 394; State of Punjab v. Mohar Singh S/o Pratap Singh AIR 1955 SC 84; T.S. Baliah v. T.S. Rangachari, ITO MANU/SC/0238/1968 : AIR 1969 SC 701; Gajraj Singh and Ors. v. State Transport Appellate Tribunal and Ors. MANU/SC/0116/1997 : (1997) 1 SCC 650; Gammon India Ltd. v. Special Chief Secretary and Ors. MANU/SC/8025/2006 : (2006) 3 SCC 354

Case Note:

FEMA - Delay - Section 19 of the Foreign Exchange Management Act, 1999 (FEMA) - Appellate Tribunal constituted under FEMA rejected belated appeal filed under Section 19 of FEMA - Hence the Appeal - Whether Appellate Tribunal constituted under the FEMA was right in rejecting a belated appeal filed under Section 19 of FEMA, applying first proviso to Section 52(2) of FERA, instead of following proviso to Section 19(2) of FEMA - Held, Section 49 of FEMA did not seek to withdraw or take away vested right of appeal in cases where proceedings were initiated prior to repeal of FERA on 1st June, 2000 or after - Procedure prescribed by FEMA only would be applicable in respect of an appeal filed under FEMA though cause of action arose under FERA - Findings rendered by Courts below that Tribunal did not have jurisdiction to condone delay beyond date prescribed under FERA was not correct understanding of law on the subject - Appellate Tribunal can entertain appeal after prescribed period of 45 days if it satisfied, that there was sufficient cause for not filing the appeal within the said period - Court set aside impugned judgments - Remitted matter back to Tribunal for fresh consideration in accordance with law - Appeal Disposed of.

Ratio Decidendi: "Procedure prescribed by FEMA only would be applicable in respect of an appeal filed under FEMA, though cause of action arose under FERA."

Industry: Chemicals

Facts:

1. The question that has come up for consideration in this case is whether the Appellate Tribunal constituted under the Foreign Exchange Management Act 1999 (in short FEMA) was right in rejecting a belated appeal filed under Section 19 of FEMA, applying the first proviso to Sub-section (2) of Section 52 of Foreign Exchange Regulation Act 1973 (in short FERA), instead of following the proviso to Sub-section (2) to Section 19 of FEMA.[2]

2. M/s Tirumalai Chemicals Limited (in short 'the Company') had imported various consignments of benezene, orthoxalene etc. for home consumption. For the said purpose, the Company had opened Letters of Credit bearing No. MLCO 4359096 and No. 529/960487 on 28.09.96 and 07.08.96 respectively on their bankers ICICI Bank and Standard Chartered Bank (authorized dealers). By letters dated 07.12.96 and 18.01.97 Exchange Control Copies of bills of entry (in short, ECC - bills of entry) in relation to those imports were forwarded by the Company to the above mentioned Banks. As per the provisions of Exchange Control Manual (in short ECM), the authorized dealers had to submit the ECC-bills of entry submitted by the importers (the Company) to the Reserve Bank of India (in short RBI). The Company was under the bonafide impression that the documents submitted by it were forwarded by the authorized dealers to the RBI and that the RBI in turn had given due intimation to the Enforcement Directorate. The Company on 22.04.2004 received a telephonic communication from the office of the 3rd Respondent viz., Directorate of Enforcement, stating that it had passed various orders on 27.01.04 imposing a total penalty of Rs. 9,33,63,453/- on the Company on the ground that it had contravened the provisions of Sections 8(3) , 8(4) of FERA read with Sub-sections (3) and (4) of

Section 49 of FEMA. Copies of the orders dated 27.01.04 were then received by the Company on 22.04.04 on request. From those orders the Company came to know that the Directorate of Enforcement had issued four show cause notices dated 14.05.02 stating that the Company had contravened Section 8(3) , Section 8(4) of FERA read with para 7A.20 (Chapter 7) of ECM and was required to show cause why adjudication proceedings be not initiated against the Company under Section 49 of FEMA for contravention of the above mentioned provisions. Further, it was also stated that the Company had failed to furnish the required bills/information/documents and did not avail of the opportunity of hearing in spite of notices issued to them on 29.08.02, 27.10.03 and 01.12.03. Orders dated 27.01.04 also indicated that an appeal would lie before the Appellate Tribunal after depositing the amount of penalty imposed within 45 days from the date on which the order was served. Reference was also made to Section 19 read with Section 49(5)(a) of FEMA.[3]

Held, while allowing the appeal

1. We, therefore, hold that the Appellate Tribunal can entertain the appeal after the prescribed period of 45 days if it is satisfied, that there was sufficient cause for not filing the appeal within the said period. We are therefore inclined to set aside the orders passed by the Tribunal and the High Court and remit the matter back to the Tribunal for fresh consideration in accordance with law on the basis of the findings recorded by us. We order accordingly. [29]

2. The appeals stand disposed of accordingly. [30]

XX

Union of India (UOI) vs. Ashok Kumar Sharma and Ors. (28.08.2020 - SC) : MANU/SC/0648/ 2020

Relative Section:

Drugs And Cosmetics Act, 1940 - Section 32; Code of Criminal Procedure, 1973 (CrPC) - Section 154;Section 190; Section 58; Drugs And Cosmetics Act, 1940 - Section 22(1)(d)

Hon'ble Judges/Coram: Sanjay Kishan Kaul and K.M. Joseph, JJ.

Equivalent Citation: AIR2020SC5274, 2020(6) ALJ 691, 2021CriLJ2006, 2020(4)Crimes13(SC), 2020 /INSC/517, 2021(3)J.L.J.R.89, 2020(4)JKJ289[SC], 2020(4)MLJ(Crl)243, 2021(3)PLJR81, 2020 (3) RCR (Criminal)726, (2021)12SCC674, [2020]10SCR923, 2020(3)UC1646

Number of Pages in the Original Judgment: 64

Case Reference:

Jeewan Kumar Raut and Ors. v. Central Bureau of Investigation MANU/SC/1153/2009; State of NCT of Delhi and Ors. v. Sanjay and Ors. MANU/SC/0761/2014; Jamiruddin Ansari v. Central Bureau of Investigation and Ors. MANU/SC/0924/2009; H.N. Rishbud and Ors. v. State of Delhi MANU/SC/

0049/1954; The Institute of Chartered Accountants of India v. Vimal Kumar Surana and Ors. MANU/SC/1015/2010; Lalita Kumari v. Govt. of U.P. and Ors. MANU/SC/1166/2013; State of Andhra Pradesh v. Punati Ramulu and Ors. MANU/SC/0417/1993; Satvinder Kaur v. State (Govt. of N.C.T. of Delhi) and Ors. MANU/SC/0632/1999; D.K. Basu v. State of West Bengal MANU/SC/0157/ 1997; Arnesh Kumar v. State of Bihar MANU/SC/0559/2014; Rini Johar and Ors. v. State of M.P. and Ors. MANU/SC/0667/2016; Badku Joti Savant v. State of Mysore MANU/SC/0276/1966; Raj Kumar Karwal and Ors. v. Union of India (UOI) and Ors. MANU/SC/0014/1991; Romesh Chandra Mehta v. State of West Bengal MANU/SC/0282/1968; Illias v. Collector of Customs, Madras MANU/SC/0297/1968; State of U.P. v. Durga Prasad MANU/SC/0216/1974; Balkishan A. Devidayal and Ors. v. State of Maharashtra and Ors. MANU/ SC/0112/1980; D. Sanjeevayya v. Election Tribunal, Andhra Pradesh and Ors. MANU/SC/0194/1967; Sultana Begum v. Prem Chand Jain MANU/SC/0227/ 1997; M. Pentiah and Ors. v. Muddala Veeramallappa and Ors. MANU/SC/ 0263/1960; Gammon India Ltd. and Ors. v. Union of India (UOI) and Ors. MANU/SC/0298/1974; Mysore State Road Transport Corporation v. Mirja Khasim Ali Beg and Ors. MANU/SC/0443/1976; V. Tulasamma and Ors. v. Sesha Reddy (Dead) by Lrs. MANU/SC/0380/1977; Punjab Beverages Pvt. Ltd., Chandigarh and Ors. v. Suresh Chand and Ors. MANU/SC/0273/1978; Commissioner of Income Tax, Central, Calcutta v. National Taj Traders MANU/SC/0310/1979; The Calcutta Gas Company (Proprietary) Ltd. v. The State of West Bengal and Ors. MANU/SC/0063/1962; The J.K. Cotton Spinning and Weaving Mills Co. Ltd. v. The State of Uttar Pradesh and Ors. MANU/SC/0287/1960; Directorate of Enforcement v. Deepak Mahajan and Ors. MANU/SC/0422/1994; Sunil Gupta v. Union of India and Ors. MANU/ PH/0106/1999; Bhavin Impex Pvt. Ltd. v. State of Gujarat MANU/GJ/0926/ 2009; Om Prakash and Ors. v. Union of India (UOI) and Ors. MANU/SC/1148/ 2011; Kanwar Pal Singh v. State of Uttar Pradesh and Anr. Criminal Appeal No. 1920 of 2019; Sanjay v. State MANU/DE/0277/2009 : (2009) 109 DRJ 594; Canada Sugar Refining Co. v. R. 1898 AC 735 : 67 LJPC 126

Case Note:

Criminal - Interplay between the provisions of the Code of Criminal Procedure (CrPC) and the Drugs and Cosmetics Act, 1940 (the Act) - Determination thereof - Whether in respect of offences falling under chapter IV of the Act, a FIR can be registered Under Section 154 of the Code of Criminal Procedure and the case investigated or whether Section 32 of the Act supplants the procedure for investigation of offences under Code of Criminal Procedure and the taking of cognizance of an offence Under Section 190 of the Code of Criminal Procedure? - Whether an Inspector under the Act can arrest a person in connection with an offence under Chapter IV of the Act?

Facts:

Upon receiving an online complaint, an inspection was carried out in concerned Clinic and Pharmacy and the Respondent No. 1 was directed to show papers in respect of medicines stored in the shop. The first Respondent according to the Appellant stated that he did not have any license though he was the owner of the medical store and that he had stored the medicines without proper license. Thereby, he allegedly committed offence Under Section 18 and 27 of the Act. On the basis of recovery made, an FIR was lodged purporting to be Under Section 18(a)(i) and Section 27 of the Act. The Respondent filed a writ petition for quashing the FIR. The Appellant was not made a party to the writ petition. The Respondents in the writ petition were the Superintendent of Police, the Station House Officer and the Drugs Inspector in his personal capacity, besides State of U.P. Appellant appeared after notice was issued by the High Court. The High Court by the impugned order allowed the writ petition and quashed the FIR, holding that under the Act Section 32 must be scrupulously observed and it is the mechanism for prosecuting offences and there is no scope for registration of a FIR under Code of Criminal Procedure.

Held, while dismissing the appeal:

The arrest of a person involves an encroachment on his personal liberty. Article 21 of the Constitution of India declares that no person shall be deprived of his personal liberty and life except in accordance with procedure established by law. There can be no doubt that the power to arrest any person therefore must be premised on a law which authorizes the same. [98]

In regard to cognizable offences under Chapter IV of the Act, in view of Section 32 of the Act and also the scheme of the Code of Criminal Procedure, the Police Officer cannot prosecute offenders in regard to such offences. Only the persons mentioned in Section 32 are entitled to do the same. There is no bar to the Police Officer, however, to investigate and prosecute the person where he has committed an offence, as stated Under Section 32(3) of the Act, i.e., if he has committed any cognizable offence under any other law. Having regard to the scheme of the Code of Criminal Procedure and also the mandate of Section 32 of the Act and on a conspectus of powers which are available with the Drugs Inspector under the Act and also his duties, a Police Officer cannot register a FIR Under Section 154 of the Code of Criminal Procedure, in regard to cognizable offences under Chapter IV of the Act and he cannot investigate such offences under the provisions of the Code of Criminal Procedure. Having regard to the provisions of Section 22(1)(d) of the Act, an arrest can be made by the Drugs Inspector in regard to cognizable offences falling under Chapter IV of the Act without any warrant and otherwise treating it as a cognizable offence. He is, however, bound by the law as laid down in D.K. Basu (supra) and to follow the provisions of Code of Criminal Procedure. It would appear that on the understanding that the Police Officer can register a FIR, there are many cases where FIRs have been registered in regard to cognizable offences falling under Chapter IV of the Act. They should be made over to the Drugs Inspectors, if not already made over, and it is for the Drugs Inspector to take action on the same in accordance with the law. In regard to the power of arrest, Police Officers do not have power to arrest in respect of cognizable offences under Chapter IV of the Act and this will operate with effect from the date of this Judgment. The Drugs Inspectors, who carry out the arrest, must not only report the arrests, as provided in Section 58 of the Code of Criminal Procedure, but also immediately report the arrests to their superior Officers. [150]

The impugned Judgment was upheld and the Appeal was dismissed. [151]
Disposition: In Favour of Accused.

XXI

Maars Software International Ltd. and Ors. vs. Union of India (UOI) and Ors. (22.04.2019 - SC) : MANU/SC/0579/2019

Relative Section:

Foreign Exchange Management Act, 1999 - Section 8,Section 13,Section 16(3),Section 35, Section 42, Section 42(1); Foreign Exchange Management (Realization, Repatriation and Surrender of Foreign Exchange) Regulations, 2000 - Regulation 3, Foreign Exchange Management (Realization, Repatriation and Surrender of Foreign Exchange) Regulations, 2000 - Regulation 9

Hon'ble Judges/Coram: Abhay Manohar Sapre and Dinesh Maheshwari, JJ.

Equivalent Citation:AIR2019SC2849, [2019]214CompCas485(SC), (2020)1CompLJ473(SC), 2019 (366) ELT598(S.C.), 2019/INSC/550, 2019(6)SCALE570, (2019)11SCC291, [2019]153SCL385(SC)

Number of Pages in the Original Judgment: 4

Case Reference: nil

Case Note:

FEMA - Violation of provision - Validity of complaint - Enforcement Directorate filed complaint, against Appellant-Company before Special Director of Enforcement - Complaint was found on material collected during course of investigation made in affairs and dealings of Appellant-Company in their business operations - Special Director allowed complaint and held that Appellant-Company had contravened provisions of FEMA and imposed penalty - On appeal, Tribunal set aside order of Special Director - On further appeal, High Court set aside order of Tribunal and restored order of Adjudicating Authority - Hence, present appeal - Whether High Court erred in setting aside order of Tribunal relating to validity of complaint.

Facts:

The Enforcement Directorate filed a complaint, under Section 16 (3) of the Foreign Exchange Management Act, 1999 against the Appellant-Company before the Special Director of Enforcement (Adjudicating Authority). The complaint was founded on the material collected during the course of detailed investigation made in the affairs and the dealings of the Appellant-Company in their business operations. The Special Director allowed the complaint and held that the Appellant-Company had contravened the provisions of FEMA and accordingly imposed a penalty. On appeal, the Tribunal set aside the order and directed the authorities to refund the amount which was deposited by the Appellants in these proceedings for filing the appeals. On further appeal, the High Court allowed the appeals, set aside the order of the Tribunal and restored the order of the Adjudicating Authority.

Held, while allowing the appeal:

(i) The Appellants had filed material, in the case, with a view to show as to what steps they had taken to realize and repatriate the dues in question. [19]

(ii) It was clear that the High Court did not examine the case of the parties in the context of material placed by the Appellants. [20]

(iii) The High Court should have taken into consideration the said material with a view to decide as to whether it was relevant or/and sufficient, and whether it could justify the Appellants' case as contemplated under Section 8 of FEMA. [21]

(iv) Instead, the High Court seemed to have proceeded on wrong assumption that since the Appellants did not file any material, a case was made out against them. This observation of the High Court, was contrary to the record of the case and hence, interference in the impugned order was called for. [22]

(v) Thus, remand the case to the High Court and request the High Court to decide the appeal afresh on merits in accordance with law. [23]

Disposition: Appeal Allowed.

Adv. Jayprakash Somani's Videos On Law

Adv. Jayprakash Somani's Videos on Law on Youtube- 'jaysomani64' channel.

1) SLP in Supreme Court / Special Leave Petitions in the Supreme Court of India

2) Transfer of Civil & Criminal Cases by the Supreme Court of India / Transfer of Matrimonial Cases

3) Appellate Jurisdiction of the Supreme Court of India

4) Jurisdictions of the Supreme Court of India

5) Public Interest Litigation in the Supreme Court of India / PIL in Supreme Court

6) Article 32 Writ Petitions in the Supreme Court of India

7) Bail Matters Top 10 Supreme Court Cases

8) FIR Quashing in High Court & Supreme Court

9) Bail & Anticipatory Bail Matters in Supreme Court

10) Insolvency & Bankruptcy Matters in the Supreme Court

11) Insolvency & Bankruptcy Code 2016 Part 1

12) Insolvency & Bankruptcy Code 2016 Part 2

13) Insolvency & Bankruptcy Code 2016 Part 3

14) Corporate Liquidation Process

15) Supreme Court Rules & Procedures Webinar of 2.5 hour on Zoom

16) RDDBFI Act, 1993 (Introduction)

17) The Indian Contact Act 1872

18) Negotiable Instruments Act (Introduction)

19) How to avoid matrimonial disputes& some more videos

20) SEBI Matters in the Supreme Court

21) Matrimonial Matters: Supreme Court's 20 Case Laws

22) Consumer Matters Supreme Court's 20 Case Laws

23) Service Matters Supreme Court's 20 Case Laws

24) How to Search Lawyer for Your Matter

25) Property Matters Supreme Court's 20 Case Laws

26) Bail Matters: Supreme Court's 20 Case Laws

27) Supreme Court / High Court Vacation Benches

28) 69000 Teacher's Recruitment Matters of UP Government in the Supreme Court

29) Contempt of Court Matters in the Supreme Court

30) Advocate Act's Matters in the Supreme Court

31) Business Law Matters in the Supreme Court

32) Banking Matters in the Supreme Court

33) Labour Law Matters in the Supreme Court

34) Arbitration Matters in the Supreme Court

35) Careers in Law -Zoom Webinar by Adv. Jayprakash Somani

36) Civil Matters in the Supreme Court

37) Consumer Protection Act | Consumer Matters in the Supreme Court

38) Corporate Matters in the Supreme Court

39) Criminal Matters in the Supreme Court

40) Role of Respondent in the Supreme Court of India

41) Motor Vehicle Accident Matters in Supreme Court with case laws

42) Article 131 Original Suits in Supreme Court

43) PIL in Supreme Court/ Public Interest Litigations in the Supreme Court of India'

44) CAB Citizenship Amendment Bill is not Unconstitutional

45) Supreme Court of India Cases & Process – Marathi

46) Legal Services Export / Export of Legal Services

47) Transfer of Matrimonial Cases by the Supreme Court of India

48) Public Interest Litigation PIL

49) The Specific Relief Act (Introduction)

50) Corporate Insolvency Resolution Process CIRP

51) ABMM's Career 5 - Careers in Law

52) Transfer of cases by Supreme Court

53) Writ Petitions in High Court & Supreme Court of India

54) Supreme Court Jurisdictions - Appeals, SLP, Writ Petitions, Transfer, Original, Review, Curative

55) LEGAL INDIA TV Show: Cases Handled in Supreme Court

56) Corporate Liquidation Process

57) Legal Services Export / Export of Legal Services

58) Corporate Laws

59) Election Matters- Supreme Court's 20 Case Laws

60) Companies Act, 2013

62) Competition Act, 2002

63) Banking Matters - Supreme Court's 20 Case Laws

64) Election Matters in the Supreme Court

65) Armed Forces Tribunal Matters in the Supreme Court

66)Compassionate Appointment Service matter

67) Foreign Exchange Management Act FEMA

68) Foreign Trade Policy 2021-26 Proposed

69) Customs Act 1962

70) Narcotic Drugs and Psychotropic Substances Act, 1985 NDPS Act

71) Foreign Trade Development & Regulation Act, 1992

72) How to Search Good Advocate in the Supreme Court of India

73) Sr. Adv Vikas Singh's Interview in Nani Palkhivala Wednesday Law Club

74) Indian Penal Code (I. P. C.)

75) Criminal Procedure Code (Cr. P. C.)

76) Commercial Courts & International Arbitration - by Mr. Jaideep Gupta, Senior Advocate in Nani Palkhivala Wednesday Law Club

77) Sr. Adv Ranji Thomos in Nani Palkhivala Wednesday Law Club

78) Urgent Matters in Supreme Court during vacations

79)498A Bail Matters in Supreme Court

81)376 Bail Matters in Supreme Court

82)302, 304, 307, 308 Bail Matters in Supreme Court

83)138, 420 Bail Matters in Supreme Court

84)POCSO Act Bail Matters in Supreme Court

85)NDPS Act Bail Matters in Supreme Court

86) What is ED (Enforcement Directorate)?

87) Prevention of Money Laundering Act, 2002 (PMLA Act)

88) Insolvency & Bankruptcy Code- Supreme Court Case Laws. Webinar in Nani Palkhivala Wednesday Law Club

89) What is NCLT & NCLAT?

90) Acquittal from 376- Supreme Court's some case laws in Nani Palkhivala Wednesday Law Club dt 28.7.22

91) Insolvency & Bankruptcy in India

92) Can we file case directly in the Supreme Court?

93) Adv. Anuja Pethia has cleared AOR Exam 2021 with 77% marks - Her interview in Nani Palkhivala Wednesday Law Club

94) Customs Act - Supreme Court Case Laws & Interview of AOR Adv. Anuja Pethia in Nani Palkhivala Law Club.

95) The Uttar Pradesh Public Service Tribunals Act, 1976

96)POCSO Act - Supreme Court Case Laws & Interview of AOR Adv. Shoumendu Mukharji & Adv. Nishant Verma in Nani Palkhivala Law Club.

97) Who Can Trigger CIRP Process Under Insolvency Law of India

98) The Uttar Pradesh Government Servant Discipline and Appeal Rules, 1999

99)CIRP Application Under Sec 7 by FC

100) Information Technology Act 2000

101) Uttar Pradesh Recruitment of Dependants of Government Servants Dying in Harness Rules, 1974

102) Foreign Exchange Management Act 1999 & Supreme Court's Case Laws on FEMA & Leading Case of AOR Exam in Nani Palkhivala Law Club.

103) Arbitration and Conciliation Act 1996 & It's Supreme Court Case Laws in Nani Palkhivala Wednesday Law Club.

104) Narcotic Drugs & Psychotropic Substances Act 1985 (NDPS Act) & It's Supreme Court Case Laws in Nani Palkhivala Wednesday Law Club.

105) Recovery of Debts and Bankruptcy Act 1993

106) Uttar Pradesh Land Revenue Code 2006

107)CIRP Application Under Sec 9 by OC

108)CIRP Application Under Sec 10 by CD

109) Hindu Succession Act, 1956

110) Maharashtra Civil Services Rules, 1981

111) Indian Contract Act, 1872 & Supreme Court's Case Laws" in Nani Palkhiwala Wednesday Law Club

112) Securities and Exchange Board of India Act, 1992 i. e. SEBI Act 1992 & Case Laws on Insiders Trading" in Nani Palkhiwala Wednesday Law Club

113) Moratorium Under Section 14 of IBC, 2016

114) Hindu Marriage Act, 1955

115) Maharashtra Land Revenue Code, 1966

116)64 Leading Cases of AOR Exam Session 1 :- Cases 1 to16 in Nani Palkhiwala Wednesday Law Club

117)64 Leading Cases of AOR Exam Session 2: Cases 17 to 32 in Nani Palkhivala Wednesday Law Club

118)64 Leading Cases of AOR Examination Session 3: Cases 33 to 48 in Nani Palkhivala Wednesday Law Club

119)64 Leading Cases of AOR Exam Session 4: Cases 49 to 64 in Nani Palkhivala Wednesday Law Club

120) Labour Laws of India: Part 1 - 4 New Labour Law Codes of India

121) New Labour Laws Part 2 The Code on Wages, 2019

122) New Labour Laws Part 3:- The Code on Social Security, 2020

123) Argue in English Fluently & Confidently - Two months online course.

124) SLP Admission in the Supreme Court. 2023 (Hindi)

125) Transfer of Petitions from the Supreme Court (Hindi)

126) Review Petition in the Supreme Court.(Hindi)

127) Recovery of debts from the Company (Hindi)

128) How to search 'Good Insolvency & Bankruptcy Consultant?' (HINDI)

129) Curative Petition in the Supreme Court

130) AFT Appeals in the Supreme Court (HINDI)

131) NCLAT's Appeals in the Supreme Court.

132) Transfer Petition: Which matters can we transfer?

133) SLP Types of SLP in the Supreme court of India (English).

134) Argue in English Fluently and Confidently in the High Court & Supreme Court'.

৪৩

List Of Adv. Jayprakash Somani's Published Books

1. Supreme Court of India's Leading Case Laws on 'Insolvency & Bankruptcy Code 2016'

2. Bail Matters – Supreme Court's Latest Leading Case Laws

3. Arbitration Matters- Supreme Court's Latest Leading Case Laws

4. Property Matters - Supreme Court's Latest Leading Case Laws

5. Matrimonial Matters- Supreme Court's Latest Leading Case Laws

6. Election Matters- Supreme Court's Latest Leading Case Laws

7. SEBI Matters- Supreme Court's Latest Leading Case Laws

8. Banking Matters- Supreme Court's Latest Leading Case Laws

9. Service Matters- Supreme Court's Latest Leading Case Laws

10. Contempt of Court Matters- Supreme Court's Latest Leading Case Laws

11. Consumer Protection Matters- Supreme Court's Latest Leading Case Laws

12. Corporate Law- Supreme Court's Latest Leading Case Laws

13. Supreme Court's AOR Exam- Leading Cases

14. Armed Force Tribunal - Supreme Court's Latest Leading Case Laws

15. Acquittal From 376 - Supreme Court's Latest Leading Case Laws

16. Negotiable instrument – Supreme Court's Latest Leading Case Laws

17. Contract Act- Supreme Court's Latest Leading Case Laws

18. Insider trading- Supreme Court's Latest Leading Case Laws

19. Foreign Exchange and Management Act- Supreme Court's Latest Leading Case Laws

20. Income Tax Act- Supreme Court's Latest Leading Case Laws

21. Company Law- Supreme Court's Latest Leading Case Laws

22. Competition & Monopoly Matters- Supreme Court's Latest Leading Case Laws

23. Compassionate Appointment- Service Matters- Supreme Court's Latest Leading Case Laws

24. Compulsory Retirement- Service Matters- Supreme Court's Latest Leading Case Laws

25. Voluntary Retirement- Service Matters- Supreme Court's Latest Leading Case Laws

26. Removal/Dismissal/Termination from Service- Supreme Court's Latest Leading Case Laws

27. Seniority- Service Matter- Supreme Court's Latest Leading Case Laws

28. Promotion- Service Matter- Supreme Court's Latest Leading Case Laws

29. Equal Pay for Equal Work- Service Matter- Supreme Court's Latest Leading Case Laws

30. Condition of Service- Service Matter- Supreme Court's Latest Leading Case Laws

31. Customs Act- Supreme Court's Leading Case Laws

32. Information Technology Act- Supreme Court's Leading Case Laws

33. SEC. 125 CR. P. C.- Supreme Court's Leading Case Laws

34. SEC. 498A OF I. P. C.- Supreme Court's Leading Case Laws

35. MOTOR VEHICLE ACT- Supreme Court's Leading Case Laws

36. CONDITION OF SERVICE- SERVICE MATTER- Supreme Court's Leading Case Laws

37. SUSPENSION- SERVICE MATTER- Supreme Court's Leading Case Laws

38. Reservation in SC, ST, OBC- Service Matter- Supreme Court's Leading Case Laws

39. NARCOTIC DRUGS AND PSYCHOTROPIC SUBSTANCES (NDPS) ACT - Supreme Court of India's Latest Leading Case Laws

40. SEC 302 IPC - Supreme Court of India's Latest Leading Case Laws

41. PROTECTION OF CHILDREN FROM SEXUAL OFFENCES ACT (POCSO) - Supreme Court of India's Latest Leading Case Laws

42. PMLA ACT BAIL MATTERS - Supreme Court of India's Leading Case Laws

43. SEC 376 BAIL MATTERS - Supreme Court of India's Leading Case Laws

44. SEC 302 BAIL MATTERS - Supreme Court of India's Leading Case Laws

45. POCSO ACT BAIL MATTERS - Supreme Court of India's Leading Case Laws

46. JUVENILE JUSTICE ACT- Supreme Court of India's Leading Case Laws

47. TRANSFER OF PROPERTY ACT- Supreme Court of India's Leading Case Laws

48. PROFESSIONAL ETHICS OF ADVOCATES- AOR EXAM- SUPREME COURT'S LEADING CASE LAWS

49. WHITE COLLAR CRIME- SUPREME COURT'S LEADING CASE LAWS

50. SEC 302 BAIL MATTERS- SUPREME COURT'S LEADING CASE LAWS

51.SEC 7 IBC 2016 - SUPREME COURT'S LATEST LEADING CASE LAW

52. ADVERSE POSSESSION IN PROPERTY MATTER - SUPREME COURT'S LATEST LEADING CASE LAWS

53. FOOD SAFETY AND STANDARD ACT 2006' - SUPREME COURT AND HIGH COURT's LEADING CASE LAWS

54.ARMED FORCE TRIBUNAL ACT- SUPREME COURT'S LATEST LEADING CASE LAWS.

55. ESSENTIAL COMMODITIES ACT 1955- SUPREME COURT'S LATEST LEADING CASE LAWS

56. FOREIGN TRADE DEVELOPMENT AND REGULATION ACT'- SUPREME COURT AND HIGH COURT'S LEADING CASE LAWS

57. PARTNERSHIP ACT 1932- SUPREME COURT'S LEADING CASE LAWS

58. COTPA ACT 2003 - SUPREME COURT AND HIGH COURT'S LEADING CASE LAWS

59. DOMESTIC VIOLENCE ACT 2005 - SUPREME COURT'S LEADING CASE LAWS

60. DOWRY PROHIBITION ACT 1961 - SUPREME COURT'S LATEST CASE LAWS

61. SUPREME COURT'S AOR EXAM- DRAFTING Formates of more than 25 Drafts for AOR Exam Paper 2 - Drafting

62. 'SPECIFIC RELIEF ACT 1963'- SUPREME COURT'S LATEST LEADING CASE LAWS

Books are available online in India

1. Notion Press: https://notionpress.com/author/jayprakash_somani

2. Amazon: https://www.amazon.in/s?k=jayprakash+somani

3. Flipkart: https://www.flipkart.com/search?q=Jayprakash%20Somani

Books are available online at International Market

4. Amazon International: https://www.amazon.com/s?k=jayprakash+somani

5. Amazon United Kingdom: https://www.amazon.co.uk/s?k=jayprakash+somani

6. E-Books/Kindle edition at National & International Level: https://www.amazon.in/s?k=jaypraksh+somani

Adv Jayprakash Somani's Online Legal & Import Export Courses

Download our app to get access to our Free Videos, Free Bare Acts, Free Study Material in Legal as well as International Business Regime.

Android App Link ;-https://clpandrea.page.link/cmSm

Ios APp Link :-https://apps.apple.com/us/app/classplus/id1324522260

Login with org code ;- (qywzji)

Web Link ;-https://qywzji.courses.store/

Download App on Google play store - Type

<u>Jayprakash Somani SupremeCourt</u>

Legal Courses :

1. SLP- Bail Matters- Drafting & Successful Arguing in the Supreme Court.
2. SLP- Succession Matters- Drafting & Successful Arguing in the Supreme Court.
3. Legal Vocabulary & its practice pattern to Argue in High Court and Supreme Court / Improve Your Legal English.

4. SLP- Property Matters - Drafting and Successful Arguing in the Supreme Court.

International Business Courses -

1. Agri Products Exports - Scope from India.
2. Textile Exports - Scope from India.
3. Export Import Procedure -Perfect Documentation & It's Management.
4. Jewellery Exports -Scope from India.
5. Export Import Finance Management with LC, ECGC & Venture Capital.
6. Shipping & Logistics in International Business with live links of Ports, ICDs, CHAs etc.
7. International Business Marketing Part 1: Finding Potential & Genuine Buyers for Exports and Suppliers for Imports.
8. International Business Marketing Part 2: Communication Skill to take repeated orders from Potential Buyers.